Traditional Knitting Patterns

Traditional
Knitting Patterns

from
Scandinavia, the British Isles, France,
Italy and other European Countries

JAMES NORBURY

DOVER PUBLICATIONS, INC
NEW YORK

Published in Canada by General Publishing Company, Ltd., 30 Lesmill Road, Don Mills, Toronto, Ontario.
Published in the United Kingdom by Constable and Company, Ltd., 10 Orange Street, London WC 2.

This Dover edition, first published in 1973, is an unabridged republication of the work first published in 1962 under the title *Traditional Knitting Patterns*. This edition is published through special arrangement with B. T. Batsford, Ltd., 4 Fitzhardinge Street, London, the original publishers. A new expanded table of contents has been prepared especially for this edition.

International Standard Book Number: 0-486-21013-8
Library of Congress Catalog Card Number: 73-79490

Manufactured in the United States of America
Dover Publications, Inc.
180 Varick Street
New York, N.Y. 10014

For Betty Morgan and Ronald Setter

My friends, we will not go again or ape an ancient rage,
Or stretch the folly of our youth to be the shame of age,
But walk with clearer eyes and ears this path that wandereth,
And see undrugged in evening light the decent inn of death;
For there is good news yet to hear and fine things to be seen,
Before we go to Paradise by way of Kensal Green.

G. K. Chesterton

Contents

INTRODUCTION

In Search of Beauty

'ART IS SKILL in making things that are useful'. In this simple dictum my friend the late Eric Gill, sounded the death-knell on the cranks and phonies who spell fine art in capital letters and common or garden craftsmanship in small ones. Some months later he enlarged upon the theme by stating categorically that, 'the artist is not a special kind of man but every man is a special kind of artist'.

Many people still think that the sanity of Gill's phrases led to the acceptance of parallels that cannot be justified in the realm of common sense. What he virtually does is equate the work of Michelangelo with the day-to-day job of the ordinary bricklayer. Surely, since Michelangelo himself was content to be called a workman, there is some justification in this suggestion. A brick properly laid is as significant as a painting, a carving or a piece of sculpture. The tragedy of our age is that we have divorced things from the places where they were meant to be, and shut them up in art galleries where at times the most beautiful objects tend to look like eccentric monstrosities because they have been divorced from their proper setting.

Once we accept the full implications of Gill's definitions, we see that the splendour of the Taj Mahal; the elegance of a Chippendale chair or a Sheraton writing-desk; the perfect shape of a Wedgwood teapot; or the fashion lines of a well-designed knitted sweater, all form an intrinsic part of the creative pattern of being called into existence by man the craftsman. They are a tribute to 'otherness', to that sense of timeless wonder that is man's true habitation.

The principles of design are basic. They cannot be classified into any specific category. The great builders of the past, those architects whose genius created the temples of Greece, the palaces of Rome, the stately homes of Florence, all called on the craftsman in gold and silver, in metal and stone, in silk and wool, to add to their basic creation those refinements that made it a thing of immortal splendour.

What are these principles? They are the simple shapes of the circle, the square, the cross and the waved line that are fundamental to all forms of design. Rooted as they are in man's thirst for divine things, they represent his finite being seeking to know and understand the meaning of infinity.

The circle, the serpent swallowing its own tail, a line that has neither beginning nor end, is the oldest symbol of eternity. The square, the formal lines of the habitation that became the home is an attempt to capture the sense of infinity in finite terms. The cross, with its four arms extending endlessly into space is the mark of the adventurous spirit that is always seeking to move from the known to the unknown, from death to life, from mortal imprisonment into that world of a being which satisfied the immortal longings within him. The waved line, the ever-recurring upsurge of the water of life that nourishes the seeds out of which the whole of creation has emerged.

This concept of design is an integral part of the true philosophy of living and doing and being. It is rooted in the primitive mystery and magic that surrounded man in the dawn time of life on this planet. These symbols were used to decorate the robes of the witch-doctors, and the vestments of the ancient priest. They mark them as being a race apart, human beings dedicated to the service of the gods and seeking to bring about the reconciliation between the known and the unknown. Later the same symbols were used to decorate the home, to remind man that this was his temporary habitation. Beyond the shadow of the walls of the cave he inhabited was a world surging with life and dominated by the haunting sense of the unknown.

The first fabrics that man produced were simple cloths made from undyed fibres out of which he created clothes for himself and hangings for his home. At a much later stage in the development of the craft of weaving, man painted simple patterns on these cloths and later still learnt how to weave the patterns into the fabric itself.

Knitted fabrics are an integral part of the development of textiles to be used in the service of man. It is not surprising, therefore, that we find in traditional knitting patterns a repetition of the principles of design that has already become part of the woven textile story.

With the rise and fall of ancient cultures designs became more complex, colours more varied and although the symbolic meaning of the patterns themselves have been lost in the mists of antiquity, the patterns still remain as part of our universal heritage.

It is interesting that in the textiles of ancient Peru; the knitted tent flaps of the early Nomads of North Africa; the magnificent knitted carpets of the Renaissance; the wonderful draperies and bedspreads made by the Dutch people in the seventeenth and eighteenth centuries; the exquisite knitted lace of France, Vienna and Shetland; the gaily decorated peasant coats of the Austrian Tyrol; the highly sophisticated sweaters of Fair Isle; all embody within themselves a common tradition.

Each little pocket of craftsmen gave their own particular twist to our story. The knitters of the Austrian Tyrol sprinkled their heavily embossed fabric with brightly coloured embroidered flowers reflecting the beauty of late spring in the Austrian valleys. The knitters of Fair Isle, inheriting their designs from Spanish sources, still preserve the Catholic tradition that made Christendom. We can still find on the sweaters they knit 'The Sacred Heart', 'The Rose of Sharon', 'The Star of Hope' and 'The Crown of Glory'.

When we move to the ice-cold wastes of Norway, we find that the fir tree and the reindeer have been copied in their woven and knitted fabrics and that even peasant costumes have been transformed into dancing figures that form border patternings on their gay sweaters. The fishermen and sailors, who were great knitters in their day, have taken the ropes and the anchors and have translated these into cable patterns and embossed designs, thus allying their day-to-day life as they go down to the sea in ships with the craft they practised in knitting jerseys to protect them from the elements.

In this book of *Traditional Knitting Patterns*, I have collected together a selection of the basic fabrics that I have found in all those parts of the world I have visited where the knitter's craft is an essential part of the life of the common people. It is surprising how the fabrics themselves reflect in some ways the temperament of their creators.

The Mediterranean countries have given us gaily coloured designs that have within them something of the laughter and sunshine that makes for the gaiety of the life of the common people. Germany and Austria present a more sombre mood, a heavier, more prosaic approach in texturing and patterning. In Holland we find a puritan simplicity and an almost stark and severe approach that reflects the sturdy and simple life of these good-hearted people. In Scandinavia, white with all the radiance of the snow is fundamental, the patterns themselves being worked in dark greens, dark reds, dark browns and dark blues, reflecting the violent contrast the snowscape presents in mid-winter.

It is through these simple truths that I have studied for over thirty years now, that I have learnt to know something of the history and habits of the common people all the world over, and it is from the universality of design, the constant recurrence of the same symbol in a different setting, that I have acquired a sense of universal kinship with all men that has become basic to my own philosophy of living.

We are all of us, like the man in Plato's cave, seeing the shadows of ourselves on the walls of our prison house and alas, all too often we mistake the shadow for the substance. The knitter's craft has taught me to have a profound respect for the aesthetic heritage that is the birthright of all mankind. It has led me to seek the Good; the best tools and the finest material out of which to create the ideas that have dominated my days; to seek the True; the perfection in line and structure that is the most perfect expression in terms of design I can find for those things I have made with my hands; to forget Beauty; knowing that if a thing is good and true then beauty can well be left to look after herself.

Abbreviations

alt.   alternate.

C.   Contrast.

C.3.   Cable 3 by slipping next 3 sts. on cable needle, leave at back, K.B.3, then K.3 across sts. on cable needle.

C.2F.   Cable 2 front by slipping next 2 sts. on cable needle, leave at front, K.2, then K.2 sts. from cable needle.

C.2B.   Cable 2 back, as above but leaving cable needle at back of work.

C.4F.   Cable 4 front by slipping next 4 sts. on to cable needle, leave at front, K.4, then K.4 from cable needle.

C.4B.   Cable 4 back, as above but leaving cable needle at back of work.

C.B.2F. & C.B.2B.   As above but working into the back of the sts. that form the cable.

C.B.3B.   Slip next 3 sts. on cable needle, leave at back, K.B.3, then K.B.3 from cable needle.

C.B.3F.   As above but leaving cable needle at front of work.

Cr.2.   Cross 2 by knitting 2 together then knit into 2nd st. before dropping st. off needle.

Cr.1F.   Cross 1 front by knitting into front of 2nd st., back of first st. then slipping both sts. off the needle.

Cr.1B.   Cross 1 back by knitting into back of 2nd st., front of first st. then slipping both sts. off the needle.

D.   Dark.

G.   Ground shade.

inc.   increase by working into front and back of stitch.

K.   Knit.

K.B.   Knit into back of stitch.

L.   Light.

M.   Main colour.

M.B.   Make bobble by purling into front and back of next st. twice, turn, K.4, turn, P.4, turn, K.4, turn, slip 2nd, 3rd and 4th st. over first st. then slip first st. on to right-hand needle.

M.1K.   Make 1 by picking up loop that lies between st. just worked and following st. and knitting into back of it.

M.1P.   Make 1 purlwise, as above but purling into back of st.

P.   Purl.

P.B.   Purl into back of stitch.

p.s.s.o.   pass slip stitch over.

rep.   repeat.

sl.   slip.

sl.1F.   slip 1 front by slipping next st. on cable needle, leave at front, P.1, then knit st. from cable needle.

sl.1B.   slip 1 back by slipping next st. on cable needle, leave at back, K.1, then purl st. from cable needle.

st.   stitch.

t.b.l.   through back of loop.

tog.   together.

Tr.1B.   Trellis 1 back by slipping next st. on to cable needle, leave at back, K.2, purl st. from cable needle.

Tr.2F.   Trellis 2 front, by slipping next 2 sts. on to cable needle, leave at front, P.1, then K.2 sts. from cable needle.

Tw.2.   Twist 2 by knitting into 2nd and first st. on left-hand needle then slip both sts. off needle together.

Tw.3.   Twist 3 by knitting into 3rd, 2nd and first st. on left-hand needle then slip all sts. off needle together.

Tw.1B.   Twist 1 back by slipping next st. on
to cable needle, leave at back, K.2,
then purl st. from cable needle.

Tw.2F.   Twist 2 front by knitting into front of
2nd st. then front of first st. on left-
hand needle then slipping 2 sts. off
needle together.

Tw.2B.   Twist 2 back by knitting into back of

2nd st. then back of first st. on left-
hand needle then slipping 2 sts. off
needle together.

w.b.   Wool back—take wool to back of
needle.

w.f.   Wool forward.

w.o.n.   Wool on needle.

w.r.n.   Wool round needle.

On Reading Charts

Knitting from charts is very simple providing
the following points are applied when working from
the chart. Each row of squares represents one row of
knitting and each square a single stitch. The odd
rows on the chart are knitted and the even rows
purled when working on two needles. All rounds are
knitted when working on four needles or more.

One important point to remember is that if you
are working from a chart and there are an odd
number of rows, in the first repeat the odd rows
are knitted and the even rows purled and in the
second repeat the odd rows are purled and the
even rows knitted.

Special Note on Colour Knitting

When coloured fabrics are being produced in
stocking stitch, the wool not in use is always
stranded across the back of the work. Where it has
to be stranded over more than five stitches it should
be twisted round the wool in use on every third
stitch thus preventing long strands at the back of
the work.

Where a number of colours are used for a
pattern, falling mainly in blocks of colour, then
what is known as Motif Knitting is the method
used. This method is to cut short lengths of wool,
as used in embroidery, using a separate length for
each colour in use and twisting the colours where
they meet to avoid gaps in the work.

I

Arabic Knitting

ARABIC KNITTING is a generic term. It covers the earliest known types of knitting that were carried out by Nomadic people living in the desert places of North Africa who were, as far as we are aware, the first knitters and are probably the antecedents of the Arabs of the present time.

The earliest known specimens of this type of knitting were all worked on frames. The frames were either circular or narrow oblong ones; the circular frames being used mainly for knitting sandal socks, the narrow oblong ones for carpets, tent flaps and possibly articles of clothing that were worn by the Tribal Leaders.

The knitting action was similar to the 'Bobbin Work' that many older readers will remember doing in the days of their own childhood. Four nails were inserted round the hole at the top of a bobbin and a cord produced by making loops on the four nails and then passing the loops singly over a length of wool that had been wound round the inside of each nail. The wool was wound round in an anti-clockwise direction producing a twisted loop, and it was from this twisted action that 'Crossed Stocking Stitch' was formed that is the basic texture of all Arabic Knitting.

When working on the frame a hook would be used to lift the loop over the twisted loop that had been placed on the peg, working in a circular motion on the round frame and in a backwards and forwards motion on the narrow oblong frame.

We do not know at what stage in the development of the craft of knitting the frames were dispensed with and the work done directly on hooked knitting needles. We do know that up to the middle of the nineteenth century hooked needles were still used in many parts of Europe and that 'Crossed Stocking Stitch' was then known as 'Continental Stocking Stitch'.

Another interesting point is seen in the difference between the English and the Continental method of knitting. In Continental Knitting the action is much more like a crochet action than a knitting one and produces a twisted stitch on the knit row but a straight stitch on the purl row, so that whereas in Arabic Knitting every pattern stitch on every row was twisted, in Continental Knitting the stitches are twisted on the knit row only.

There is one other point of historical interest that is worthy of note. In knitted fabrics produced by a method known as Peruvian Needle Knitting, we find a similarity in design to Arabic Knitting. This is probably due to the fact that knitting was taken to Spain from Africa by the early traders and from Spain to South America at the time of the conquest of Mexico and Peru. Hence we find that early Spanish Knitting and pre-Columbian Knitting in South America bear a marked similarity in design to Arabic Knitting.

I

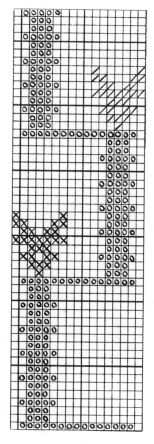

2

3

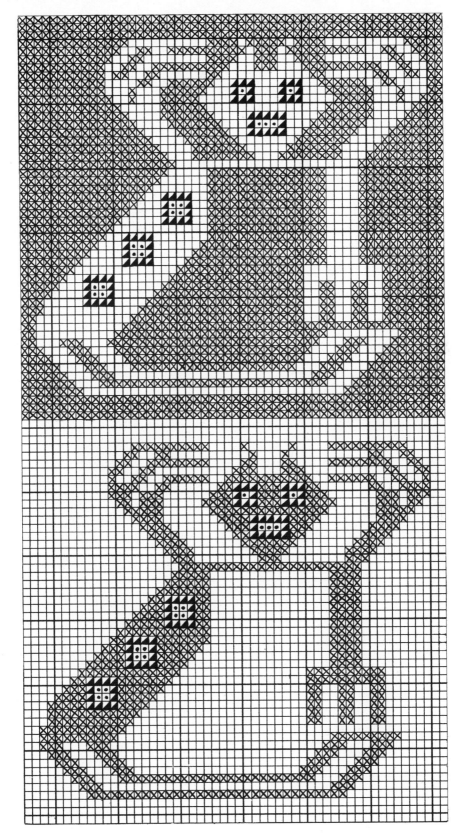

3

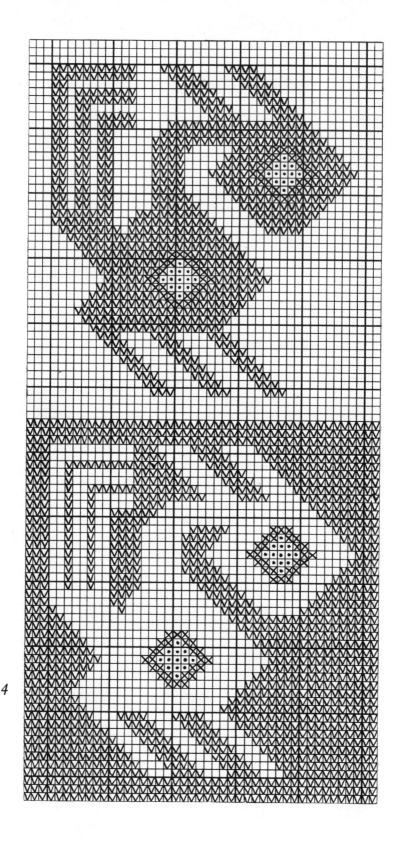

4

ARABIC

4

ARABIC

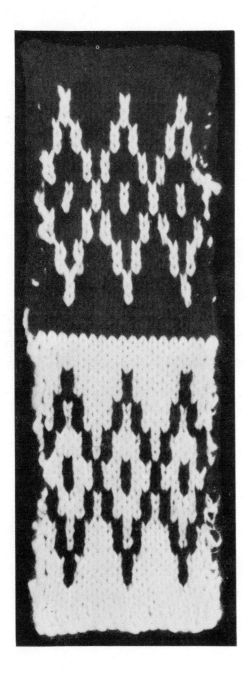

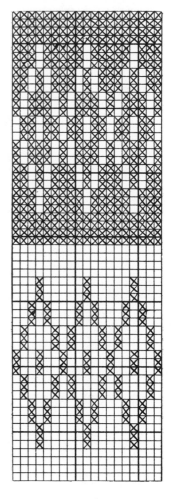

5

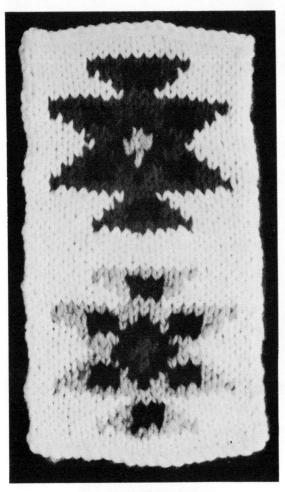

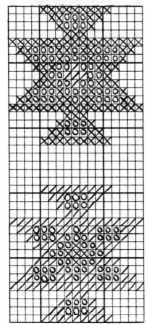

6

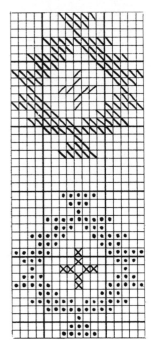

7

8

ARABIC

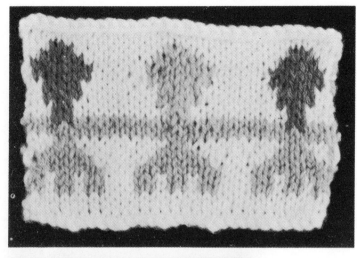

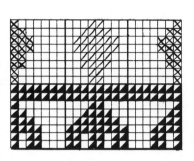

9

10

ARABIC KNITTING PATTERNS

Crossed Stocking Stitch Pattern

1st row   K.B. all across.

2nd row   Purl all across.

11

Embossed Diamond Pattern
Multiple of 8 + 1

12

1st row   Purl.

2nd row   Knit.

3rd row   + P.4, K.B.1, P.3, rep. from + P.1.

4th row   + K.4, P.B.1, K.3, rep. from + K.1.

5th row   + P.3, K.B.3, P.2, rep. from + P.1.

6th row   + K.3, P.B.3, K.2, rep. from + K.1.

7th row   + P.2, K.B.5, P.1, rep. from + P.1.

8th row   + K.2, P.B.5, K.1, rep. from + K.1.

9th & 10th rows   As 5th & 6th.

11th & 12th rows   As 3rd & 4th.

These 12 rows form the pattern

Embossed Cross Stitch Pattern

Multiple of 12 + 1

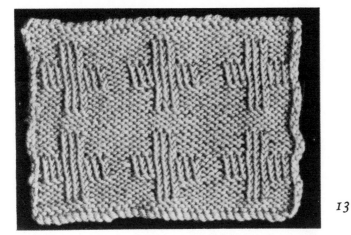

13

1st row Purl.	*7th row* + P.2, K.B.9, P.1, rep. from + P.1.
2nd row Knit.	*8th row* + K.2, P.B.9, K.1, rep. from + K.1.
3rd row + P.5, K.B.3, P.4, rep. from + P.1.	*9th & 10th rows* As 7th & 8th.
4th row + K.5, P.B.3, K.4, rep. from + K.1.	*11th–14th rows* Rep. 3rd & 4th twice.
5th & 6th rows As 3rd & 4th.	*15th & 16th rows* As 1st & 2nd.

These 16 rows form the pattern

Embossed Chequer Pattern

Multiple of 10 + 1

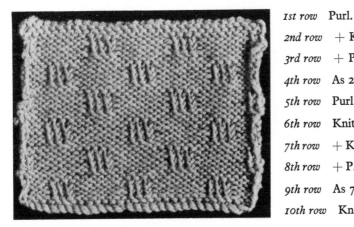

1st row Purl.

2nd row + K.4, P.B.3, K.3, rep. from + K.1.

3rd row + P.4, K.B.3, P.3, rep. from + P.1.

4th row As 2nd.

5th row Purl.

6th row Knit.

7th row + K.B.2, P.7, K.B.1, rep. from + K.B.1.

8th row + P.B.2, K.7, P.B.1, rep. from + P.B.1.

9th row As 7th.

10th row Knit.

These 10 rows form the pattern

14

Embossed Pennant Pattern

Multiple of 6

15

1st row	K.B.1, P.5.	*4th row*	K.2, P.B.4.
2nd row	K.4, P.B.2.	*5th row*	K.B.5, P.1.
3rd row	K.B.3, P.3.	*6th, 7th & 8th rows*	As 4th, 3rd & 2nd.

These 8 rows form the pattern

Chequer and Diagonal Pattern

Multiple of 8 + 4

1st row K.B., all across.

2nd row P.B.4, + K.4, P.B.4, rep. from + to end.

3rd row + P.1, K.B.4, P.3, rep. from + P.1, K.B.3.

4th row P.B.2, K.2, + K.2, P.B.4, K.2, rep. from + to end.

5th row + P.3, K.B.4, P.1, rep. from + P.3, K.B.1.

6th row K.4, + P.B.4, K.4, rep. from + to end.

7th row K.B., all across.

8th row P.B.4, + K.4, P.B.4, rep. from + to end.

9th row + K.B.4, P.4, rep. from + K.B.4.

10th & 11th rows As 8th & 9th.

12th row P.B., all across.

13th row + P.4, K.B.4, rep. from + P.4.

16

14th row P.B.1, K.3, + K.1, P.B.4, K.3, rep. from + to end.

15th row + P.2, K.B.4, P.2, rep. from + P.2, K.B.2.

16th row P.B.3, K.1, + K.3, P.B.4, K.1, rep. from + to end.

17th row + K.B.4, P.4, rep. from + K.B.4.

18th row P.B., all across.

19th row + P.4, K.B.4, rep. from + P.4.

20th row K.4, + P.B.4, K.4, rep. from + to end.

21st & 22nd rows As 19th & 20th.

These 22 rows form the pattern

II

Spanish Knitting

ALTHOUGH we have no exact knowledge as to when knitting arrived in Spain from North Africa, we do know that by the ninth century it was a flourishing craft in that country.

In the Ashmolean Museum in Oxford there is a wonderful example of a Spanish Altar Glove knitted in the ninth century. At a first glance this glove appears to have been made from a piece of magnificent brocade but when we examine it carefully we find that it has been knitted in 'Crossed Stocking Stitch', thus following the Arabic tradition, and is in fine silks of many colours with gold and silver threads introduced into the knitting.

It is highly probable that most of the knitting done in Spain during the early centuries of the Christian era, was carried out in the service of the Catholic Church. The Altar Gloves referred to are a perfect example of this and in several places in Spain there are wonderful examples of knitted Altar Frontals.

It is also possible that we owe the origin of Lace Knitting to the Spanish tradition. The names of some of the patterns themselves are evidence of this fact.

17

18

SPANISH

18

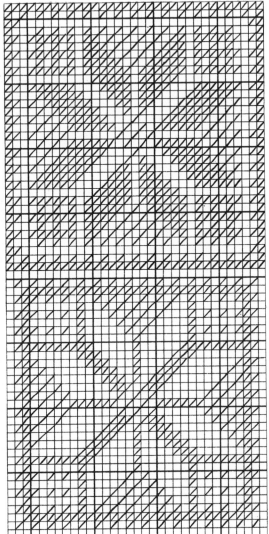

19

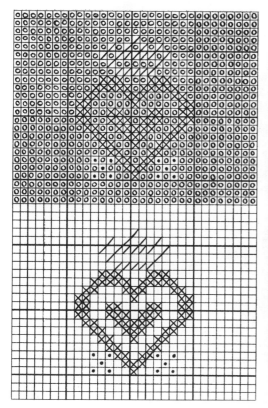

20

SPANISH

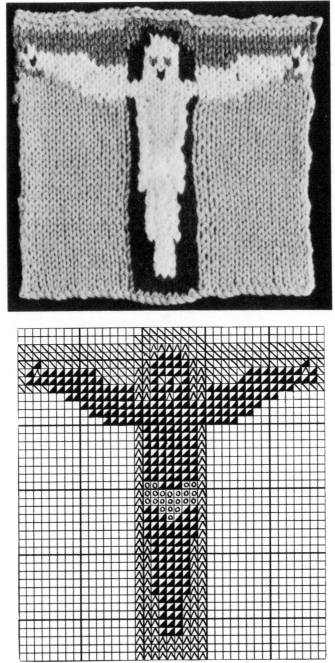

21

SPANISH KNITTING PATTERNS

Madeira Leaf Stitch Border Pattern

Multiple of 10 + 4

22

1st row   Knit.

2nd row   Purl.

3rd–6th rows   Rep. 1st & 2nd twice.

7th row   K.2, + w.f., K.2 tog. t.b.l., K.8, rep. from + K.2.

8th row   K.2, + K.7, P.2 tog. t.b.l., w.r.n., P.1, rep. from + K.2.

9th row   K.2, + (w.f., K.2 tog. t.b.l.) twice, K.6, rep. from + K.2.

10th row   K.2, + K.5, P.2 tog. t.b.l., w.r.n., P.2, K.1, rep. from + K.2.

11th row   K.2, + (K.1, w.f., K.2 tog. t.b.l.) twice, K.4, rep. from + K.2.

12th row   K.2, + K.3, P.2 tog. t.b.l., w.r.n., P.3, K.2, rep. from + K.2.

13th row   K.2, + (K.2, w.f., K.2 tog. t.b.l.) twice, K.2, rep. from + K.2.

14th row   K.2, + K.1, P.2 tog. t.b.l., w.r.n., P.4 K.3, rep. from + K.2.

15th row   K.2, + (K.3, w.f., K.2 tog. t.b.l.) twice, rep. from + K.2.

16th row   K.2, + P.4, P.2 tog. t.b.l., w.o.n., K.4, rep. from + K.2.

17th row   K.3, + K.4, w.f., K.2 tog. t.b.l., K.2, w.f., K.2, tog. t.b.l., rep. from + K.1.

18th row   K.2, + P.2, P.2 tog. t.b.l., w.o.n., K.5, P.1, rep. from + K.2.

19th row   K.2, + w.f., K.2 tog. t.b.l., K.5, w.f., K.2 tog. t.b.l., K.1, rep. from + K.2.

20th row   K.2, + P.2 tog. t.b.l., w.o.n., K.6, P.2, rep. from + K.2.

21st row   K.3, + w.f., K.2 tog. t.b.l., K.6, w.f., K.2 tog. t.b.l., rep. from + K.1.

22nd row K.2, + K.7, P.1, P.2 tog. t.b.l., w.o.n., rep. from + K.2.

23rd row K.2, + K.1, w.f., K.2 tog. t.b.l., K.7, rep. from + K.2.

24th & 26th rows Knit.

25th row K.2, + w.f., K.2 tog. t.b.l., rep. from + K.2.

27th row K.2, + K.2 tog., w.f., K.8, rep. from + K.2.

28th row K.1, + w.r.n., P.2 tog., K.7, P.1, rep. from + w.r.n., P.2 tog., K.1.

29th row K.2, + P.2 tog., w.o.n., K.6, K.2 tog., w.r.n., rep. from + K.2.

30th row K.2, + P.1, w.r.n., P.2 tog., K.6, P.1, rep. from + K.2.

31st row K.1, + K.2 tog., w.f., K.5, K.2 tog., w.f., K.1, rep. from + K.3.

32nd row K.2, + P.3, w.r.n., P.2 tog., K.5, rep. from + K.2.

33rd row K.2, + K.4, K.2 tog., w.f., K.2, K.2 tog., w.f., rep. from + K.2.

34th row K.2, + K.1, P.4, w.r.n., P.2 tog., K.3, rep. from + K.2.

35th row K.2, + K.2, K.2 tog., w.f., K.3, K.2 tog., w.f., K.1, rep. from + K.2.

36th row K.2, + K.2, w.r.n., P.2 tog., P.4, K.2, rep. from + K.2.

37th row K.2, + K.1, K.2 tog., w.f., K.2, K.2 tog., w.f., K.3, rep. from + K.2.

38th row K.2, + K.4, w.r.n., P.2 tog., P.3, K.1, rep. from + K.2.

39th row K.2, + K.2 tog., w.f., K.1, K.2 tog., w.f., K.5, rep. from + K.2.

40th row K.2, + K.6, w.r.n., P.2 tog., P.2, rep. from + K.2.

41st row K.1, + (K.2 tog., w.f.) twice, K.6, rep. from + K.3.

42nd row K.2, + P.1, K.7, w.r.n., P.2 tog., rep. from + K.2.

43rd row K.1, + K.2 tog., w.f., K.8, rep. from + K.3.

44th row Purl.

45th row Knit.

46th–49th rows Rep. 44th & 45th twice.

These 49 rows form the pattern

Square Medallion (1)

With Ground Shade

23

Cast on 2 sts. on each of 4 needles.

Each set of instructions followed by + is to be worked four times.

1st round and every other round to the 43rd round and 49th round. Knit throughout.

2nd round W.f., K.1, w.f., K.1, +.

4th round W.f., K.1, w.f., sl.1, K.1, p.s.s.o., w.f., K.1, +.

6th round W.f., K.2 tog., w.f., K.1, w.f., sl.1, K.1, p.s.s.o., w.f., K.1, +.

8th round W.f., K.2, w.r.n., P.3 tog., w.o.n., K.2, w.f., K.1, +.

10th round W.f., K.1, K.2 tog., w.f., K.3, w.f., Sl.1, K.1, p.s.s.o., K.1, w.f., K.1, +.

12th round W.f., K.3, w.f., K.1, P.3 tog., K.1, w.f., K.3, w.f., K.1, +.

14th round W.f., K.2, K.2 tog., w.f., K.5, w.f., sl.1, K.1, p.s.s.o., K.2, w.f., K.1, +.

16th round W.f., K.4, w.f., K.2, P.3 tog., K.2, w.f., K.4, w.f., K.1, +.

18th round W.f., K.3, K.2 tog., w.f., K.7, w.f., sl.1, K.1, p.s.s.o., K.3, w.f., K.1, +.

20th round W.f., K.5, w.f., K.3, P.3 tog., K.3, w.f., K.5, w.f., K.1, +.

22nd round W.f., K.4, K.2 tog., w.f., K.9, w.f., sl.1, K.1, p.s.s.o., K.4, w.f., K.1, +.

24th round W.f., K.6, w.f., K.4, P.3 tog., K.4, w.f., K.6, w.f., K.1, +.

26th round W.f., K.5, K.2 tog., w.f., K.11, w.f., sl.1, K.1, p.s.s.o., K.5, w.f., K.1, +.

28th round W.f., K.7, w.f., K.5, P.3 tog., K.5, w.f., K.7, w.f., K.1, +.

30th round W.f., K.6, K.2 tog., w.f., K.1, w.f., sl.1, K.1, p.s.s.o., K.7, K.2 tog., w.f., K.1, w.f., sl.1, K.1, p.s.s.o., K.6, w.f., K.1, +.

32nd round W.f., K.6, K.2 tog., w.f., K.3, w.f., sl.1, K.1, p.s.s.o., K.5, K.2 tog., w.f., K.3, w.f., sl.1, K.1, p.s.s.o., K.6, w.f., K.1, +.

34th round W.f., K.1, w.f., ++ sl.1, K.1, p.s.s.o., K.3, K.2 tog., w.f., K.1, w.f., sl.1, K.2 tog., p.s.s.o., w.f., K.1, w.f., rep. once from ++; sl.1, K.1, p.s.s.o., K.3, K.2 tog., w.f., K.1, w.f., K.1, +.

36th round W.f., K.3, w.f., ++ sl.1, K.1, p.s.s.o., K.1, K.2 tog., w.f., K.3, w.f., sl.1, K.1, p.s.s.o., K.2, w.f., rep. once from ++; sl.1, K.1, p.s.s.o., K.1, K.2 tog., w.f., K.3, w.f., K.1, +.

38th round ++ W.f., K.1, w.f., sl.1, K.2 tog., p.s.s.o., rep. from ++ 8 times; w.f., K.1, w.f., K.1, +.

40th round W.f., K.3, ++ w.f., Sl.1, K.1, p.s.s.o., K.2, rep. from ++ 8 times; w.f., K.1, +.

42nd round ++ W.f., K.1, w.f., Sl.1, K.2 tog., p.s.s.o., rep. from ++ 9 times; w.f., K.1, w.f., K.1, +.

44th round With C: w.f., K.43, w.f., K.1, +.

45th, 46th, 51st, 52nd, 57th & 58th rounds With C: P. throughout.

47th round With G: w.f., K.45, w.f., K.1, +.

48th round With G: w.f., K.1, ++ w.f., sl.1, K.1, p.s.s.o., rep from ++ 22 times, w.f., K.1, +.

50th round With C: w.f., K.49, w.f., K.1, +.

53rd round With C: w.f., K.51, w.f., K.1, +.

54th round With C: w.f., K.1, ++ w.f., sl.1, K.1, p.s.s.o., rep. from ++ 25 times, w.f., K.1, +.

55th round With C: Knit.

56th round With C: w.f., K.55, w.f., K.1, +.

These 56 rounds complete the pattern

Square Medallion (2)

24

With G., cast on 2 sts. on each of four needles. Each set of instructions followed by + is to be worked four times.

1st round W.f., K.1, w.f., K.1, +.

Every even-numbered round, from 2nd to the 48th and the 56th round. K. throughout.

3rd round   W.f., K.3, w.f., K.1, +.

5th round   W.f., K.5, w.f., K.1, +.

7th round   W.f., K.7, w.f., K.1, +.

9th round   W.f., K.9, w.f., K.1, +.

11th round   W.f., K.11, w.f., K.1, +.

13th round   W.f., K.13, w.f., K.1, +.

15th round   W.f., K.1, ++ w.f., sl.1, K.1, p.s.s.o, rep. once from ++, w.f., sl.1, K.2 tog., p.s.s.o., +++ w.f., K.2 tog., rep. once from +++, w.f., K.2 tog., w.f., K.1, w.f., K.1, +.

17th round   W.f., K.3, ++ w.f., sl.1, K.1, p.s.s.o., rep. once from ++, w.f., sl.1, K.2 tog., p.s.s.o., +++ w.f., K.2 tog., rep. once from +++, w.f., K.3, w.f., K.1, +.

19th round   W.f., K.5. w.f., sl.1, K.1, p.s.s.o., w.f., sl.1, K.2 tog., p.s.s.o., ++ w.f., K.2 tog., rep. once from ++, w.f., K.5, w.f., K.1, +.

21st round   W.f., K.7, w.f., sl.1, K.1, p.s.s.o., w.f., sl.1, K.2 tog., p.s.s.o., w.f., K.2 tog., w.f., K.7, w.f., K.1, +.

23rd round   W.f., K.2, K.2 tog., w.f., K.1, w.f., sl.1, K.1, p.s.s.o., K.2, w.f., sl.1, K.2 tog., p.s.s.o., w.f., K.2 tog.; w.f., K.2, K.2 tog., w.f., K.1, w.f., sl.1, K.1, p.s.s.o., K.2, w.f., K.1, +.

25th round   W.f., K.2, K.2 tog., w.f., K.3, w.f., sl.1, K.1, p.s.s.o., K.2, w.f., sl.1, K.2 tog., p.s.s.o., w.f., K.2, K.2 tog., w.f., K.3, w.f., sl.1, K.1, p.s.s.o., K.2, w.f., K.1, +.

27th round   W.f., K.2, ++ K.2 tog., w.f., rep. once from ++, K.1, +++ w.f., sl.1, K.1, p.s.s.o., rep. once from +++, K.5, ++++ K.2 tog., w.f., rep. once from ++++, K.1, +++++ w.f., sl.1, K.1, p.s.s.o., rep. once from +++++, K.2, w.f., K.1, +.

29th round   W.f., K.2, ++ K.2 tog., w.f., rep. once from ++, K.3, +++ w.f., sl.1, K.1, p.s.s.o., rep. once from +++, K.3, ++++ K.2 tog., w.f., rep. once from ++++, K.3, +++++ w.f., sl.1, K.1, p.s.s.o., rep. once from +++++, K.2, w.f., K.1, +.

31st round   W.f., K.2, ++ K.2 tog., w.f., rep. twice from ++, K.1, +++ w.f., sl.1, K.1,

p.s.s.o., rep. twice from +++, K.1, ++++ K.2 tog., w.f., rep. twice from ++++, K.1, +++++ w.f., sl.1, K.1, p.s.s.o., rep. twice from +++++, K.2, w.f., K.1, +.

33rd round   W.f., K.4, ++ K.2 tog., w.f., rep. once from ++, K.3, +++ w.f., sl.1, K.1, p.s.s.o., rep. once from +++, K.3, ++++ K.2 tog., w.f., rep. once from ++++, K.3, +++++ w.f., sl.1, K.1, p.s.s.o., rep. once from +++++, K.4, w.f., K. 1, +.

35th round   W.f., K.6, ++ K.2 tog., w.f., rep. once from ++, K.1, +++ w.f., sl.1, K.1, p.s.s.o., rep. once from +++, K.5, ++++ K.2 tog., w.f., rep. once from ++++, K.1, +++++ w.f., sl.1, K.1, p.s.s.o., rep. once from +++++, K.6, w.f., K.1, +.

37th round   W.f., K.8, K.2 tog., w.f., K.3, w.f., sl.1, K.1, p.s.s.o., K.7, K.2 tog., w.f., K.3, w.f., sl.1, K.1, p.s.s.o., K.8, w.f., K.1, +.

39th round   W.f., K.8, ++ K.2 tog., w.f., rep. once from ++, K.1, +++ w.f., sl.1, K.1, p.s.s.o., rep. once from +++, K.5, ++++ K.2 tog., w.f., rep. once from ++++, K.1, +++++ w.f., sl.1, K.1, p.s.s.o., rep. once from +++++, K.8, w.f., K.1, +.

41st round   W.f., K.8, ++ K.2 tog., w.f., rep. once from ++, K.3, +++ w.f., sl.1, K.1, p.s.s.o., rep. once from +++, K.3, ++++ K.2 tog., w.f., rep. once from ++++, K.3, +++++ w.f., sl.1, K.1, p.s.s.o., rep. once from +++++, K.8, w.f., K.1, +.

43rd round   W.f., K.10, ++ K.2 tog., w.f., rep. once from ++, K.1, +++ w.f., sl.1, K.1, p.s.s.o., rep. once from +++, K.5, ++++ K.2 tog., w.f., rep. once from ++++, K.1, +++++ w.f., sl.1, K.1, p.s.s.o., rep. once from +++++, K.10, w.f., K.1, +.

45th round   W.f., K.12, K.2 tog., w.f., K.3, w.f., sl.1, K.1, p.s.s.o., K.7, K.2 tog., w.f., K.3, w.f., sl.1, K.1, p.s.s.o., K.12, w.f., K.1. +.

47th round   W.f., K.14, K.2 tog., w.f., K.1, w.f., sl.1, K.1, p.s.s.o., K.9, K.2 tog., w.f., K.1, w.f., sl.1, K.1, p.s.s.o., K.14, w.f., K.1, +.

49th round   With C: w.f., K.49, w.f., K.1, +.

50th, 52nd, 54th, 58th, 60th & 62nd rounds With C: P. throughout.

51st round With C: w.r.n., P. 51, w.r.n., P.1, +.

53rd round With C: w.r.n., P. 53, w.r.n., P.1, +.

55th round With G: w.f., K.55, w.f., K.1, +.

57th round With C: w.f., K.57, w.f., K.1, +.

59th round With C: w.r.n., P.59, w.r.n., P.1, +.

61st round With C: w.r.n., P.61, w.r.n., P.1, +.

These 61 rounds complete the pattern

Diagonal Lace Madeira Pattern

Multiple of 8 + 4

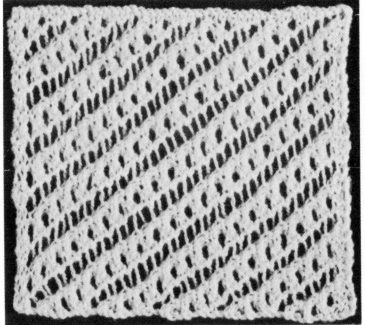

25

1st row K.2, + w.r.n., P.2 tog., K.1, P.2 tog., w.o.n., K.3, rep. from + K.2.

2nd row K.2, + K.5, P.2 tog., w.o.n., K.1, rep. from + K.2.

3rd row K.2, + K.2, w.r.n., P.2 tog., K.1, P.2 tog., w.o.n., K.1, rep. from + K.2.

4th row K.2, + K.3, P.2 tog., w.o.n., K.3, rep. from + K.2.

5th row K.1, + P.2 tog., w.o.n., K.3, w.r.n., P.2 tog., K.1. rep. from + K.3.

6th row K.2. + K.1, P.2 tog., w.o.n., K.5, rep. from + K.2.

7th row K.2, + K.1, P.2 tog., w.o.n., K.3, w.r.n., P.2 tog., rep. from + K.2.

8th row K.1, + P.2 tog., w.o.n., K.6, rep. from + K.3.

These 8 rows form the pattern

Vandyke Madeira Pattern

Multiple of 8 + 4

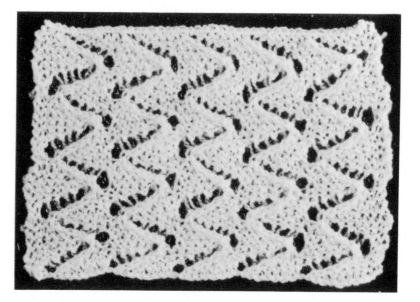

26

1st row K.2, + K.6, K.2 tog., w.f., rep. from + K.2.

2nd row K.2, + K.1, w.r.n., P.2 tog., K.5, rep. from + K.2.

3rd row K.2, + K.4, K.2 tog., w.f., K.2, rep. from + K.2.

4th row K.2, + K.3, w.r.n., P.2 tog., K.3, rep. from + K.2.

5th row K.2, + K.2, K.2 tog., w.f., K.4, rep. from + K.2.

6th row K.2, + K.5, w.r.n., P.2 tog., K.1, rep. from + K.2.

7th row K.2, + K.2 tog., w.f., K.6, rep. from + K.2.

8th row K.2, + K.6, P.2 tog. t.b.l., w.o.n., rep. from + K.2.

9th row K.2, + K.1, w.f., K.2 tog. t.b.l., K.5, rep. from + K.2.

10th row K.2, + K.4, P.2 tog. t.b.l., w.o.n., K.2, rep. from + K2.

11th row K.2, + K.3, w.f., K.2 tog. t.b.l., K.3, rep, from + K.2.

12th row K.2, + K.2, P.2 tog. t.b.l., w.o.n., K.4, rep. from + K.2.

13th row K.2, + K.5, w.f., K.2 tog. t.b.l., K.1, rep. from + K.2.

14th row K.2, + P.2 tog. t.b.l., w.o.n., K.6, rep. from + K.2.

These 14 rows form the pattern

Madeira Mesh Pattern

Multiple of 6 + 7

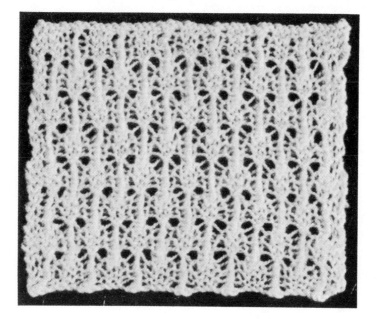

27

1st–6th rows   K.2, + w.r.n., P.3 tog., w.o.n., K.3, rep. from + w.r.n., P.3 tog., w.o.n., K.2.

7th–12th rows   K.2, + K.3, w.r.n., P.3 tog., w.o.n., rep. from + K.5.

These 12 rows form the pattern

Madeira Mesh Diamond Stitch Pattern

Multiple of 8 + 4

1st row   K.2, + w.f., K.2 tog. t.b.l., K.6, rep. from + K.2.

2nd row   K.2, + w.r.n., P.2 tog., K.3, P.2 tog. t.b.l., w.o.n., K.1, rep. from + K.2.

3rd row   K.2, + K.2, w.f., K.2 tog. t.b.l., K.1, K.2 tog., w.f., K.1, rep. from + K.2.

4th row   K.2, + K.2, w.r.n., P.3 tog. t.b.l., w.o.n., K.3, rep. from + K.2.

28

5th row K.2, + K.4, w.f., K.2 tog. t.b.l., K.2, rep. from + K.2.

6th row K.2, + K.1, P.2 tog. t.b.l., w.o.n., K.1, w.r.n., P.2 tog., K.2, rep. from + K.2.

7th row K.2, + K.1, K.2 tog., w.f., K.3, w.f., K.2 tog. t.b.l., rep. from + K.2.

8th row K.1, P.2 tog. t.b.l., + w.o.n., K.5, w.r.n., P.3 tog. t.b.l., rep. from + w.o.n., K.5, w.r.n., P.2 tog., K.2.

These 8 rows form the pattern

Madeira Cascade Pattern

Multiple of 20 + 5

1st, 4th, 6th, 8th, 10th, 12th, 14th, 16th, 18th rows K.2, P. to last 2 sts., K.2.

2nd row Knit.

3rd row K.2, + K.1, w.f., K.8, P.3 tog., K.8, w.f., rep. from + K.3.

5th row K.2, + K.2, w.f., K.7, P.3 tog., K.7, w.f., K.1, rep. from + K.3.

7th row K.2, K.2 tog., + w.f., K.1, w.f., K.6, P.3 tog., K.6, w.f., K.1, w.f., Sl.1, K.2 tog., p.s.s.o., rep. from + w.f., K.1, w.f., K.6, P.3 tog., K.6, w.f., K.1, w.f., K.2 tog. t.b.l., K.2.

9th row K.2, + K.4, w.f., K.5, P.3 tog., K.5, w.f., K.3, rep. from + K.3.

29

11th row K.2, + K.1, w.f., sl.1, K.2 tog., p.s.s.o., w.f., K.1, w.f., K.4, P.3 tog., K.4, w.f., K.1, w.f., sl.1, K.2 tog., p.s.s.o., w.f., rep. from + K.3.

13th row K.2, + K.6, w.f., K.3, P.3 tog., K.3, w.f., K.5, rep. from + K.3.

15th row K.2, K.2 tog., + w.f., K.1, w.f., sl.1, K.2 tog., p.s.s.o., w.f., K.1, w.f., K.2, P.3 tog., K.2, w.f., K.1, w.f., sl.1, K.2 tog., p.s.s.o., w.f., K.1, w.f., sl.1, K.2 tog., p.s.s.o., rep. from + w.f., K.1, w.f., sl.1, K.2 tog., p.s.s.o., w.f., K.1,

w.f., K.2, P.3 tog., K.2, w.f., K.1, w.f., sl.1, K.2 tog., p.s.s.o., w.f., K.1, w.f., K.2 tog. t.b.l., K.2.

17th row K.2, + K.8, w.f., K.1, P.3 tog., K.1, w.f., K.7, rep. from + K.3.

19th row K.2, + K.1, (w.f., sl.1, K.2 tog., p.s.s.o., w.f., K.1) twice, w.r.n., P.3 tog., w.o.n., (K.1, w.f., sl.1, K.2 tog., p.s.s.o., w.f.) twice, rep. from + K.3.

20th row Knit.

These 20 rows form the pattern

45

Insertion

Cast on 32 sts.

1st–6th, 19th–24th, 27th, 28th, 31st, 32nd, 35th, 36th, 39th, 40th, 43rd–48th, 61st–66th, 69th, 70th, 73rd, 74th, 77th, 78th, 81st & 82nd rows Sl.1, K.3, w.f., sl.1, K.1, p.s.s.o., K.22, w.f., sl.1, K.1, p.s.s.o., K.2.

7th–18th, 49th–60th rows Sl.1, K.1, + K.2, w.f., sl.1, K.1, p.s.s.o., rep. from + 6 times, K.2.

25th & 83rd rows Sl.1, K.3, w.f., sl.1, K.1, p.s.s.o., + w.f., K.2 tog., w.f., sl.1, K.1, p.s.s.o., rep. twice from + K.10, w.f., sl.1, K.1, p.s.s.o., K.2.

26th & 84th rows Sl.1, K.3, w.f., sl.1, K.1, p.s.s.o., K.10, + P.1, K.3, rep. once from +, P.1, K.3, w.f., sl.1, K.1, p.s.s.o., K.2.

29th & 79th rows Sl.1, K.3, w.f., sl.1, K.1, p.s.s.o., K.2, + K.2 tog., (w.f.) twice, sl.1, K.1, p.s.s.o., rep. twice from + K.8, w.f., sl.1, K.1, p.s.s.o., K.2.

30th & 80th rows Sl.1, K.3, w.f., sl.1, K.1, p.s.s.o., K.8, + P.1, K.3, rep. once from +, P.1, K.5, w.f., sl.1, K.1, p.s.s.o., K.2.

33rd & 75th rows Sl.1, K.3, w.f., sl.1, K.1, p.s.s.o., K.4, + K.2 tog., (w.f.) twice, sl.1, K.1, p.s.s.o., rep. twice from +, K.6, w.f., sl.1, K.1, p.s.s.o., K.2.

34th & 76th rows Sl.1, K.3, w.f., sl.1, K.1, p.s.s.o., K.6, + P.1, K.3, rep. once from +, P.1, K.7, w.f., sl.1, K.1, p.s.s.o., K.2.

37th & 71st rows Sl.1, K.3, w.f., sl.1, K.1, p.s.s.o., K.6, + K.2 tog., (w.f.) twice, sl.1, K.1, p.s.s.o., rep. twice from +, K.4, w.f., sl.1, K.1, p.s.s.o., K.2.

38th & 72nd rows Sl.1, K.3, w.f., sl.1, K.1, p.s.s.o., K.4, + P.1, K.3, rep. once from +, P.1, K.9, w.f., sl.1, K.1, p.s.s.o., K.2.

41st & 67th rows Sl.1, K.3, w.f., sl.1, K.1, p.s.s.o., K.8, + K.2 tog., (w.f.) twice, sl.1, K.1, p.s.s.o., rep. twice from +, K.2, w.f., sl.1, K.1, p.s.s.o., K.2.

42nd & 68th rows Sl.1, K.3, w.f., sl.1, K.1, p.s.s.o., K.2, + P.1, K.3, rep. once from +, P.1, K.11, w.f., sl.1, K.1, p.s.s.o., K.2.

Rep. from the 1st row.

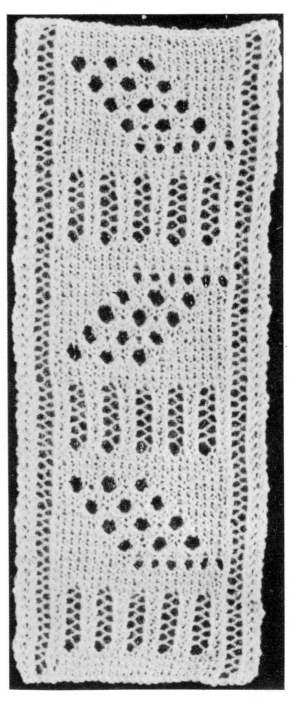

30

46

Madeira Wave Stitch Pattern

Multiple of 12 + 5

31

1st & 29th rows K.2, + w.f., K.2 tog. t.b.l., K.10, rep. from + w.f., K.2 tog. t.b.l., K.1.

2nd row K.2, + P.2, K.9, P.1, rep. from + P.1, K.2.

3rd & 31st rows K.2, + K.1, w.f., K.2 tog. t.b.l., K.7, K.2 tog., w.f., rep. from + K.3.

4th row K.2, + P.3, K.7, P.2, rep. from + P.1, K.2.

5th & 33rd rows K.2, + K.2, w.f., K.2 tog. t.b.l., K.5, K.2 tog., w.f., K.1, rep. from + K.3.

6th row K.2, + P.4, K.5, P.3, rep. from + P.1, K.2.

7th & 35th rows K.2, + K.3, w.f., K.2 tog. t.b.l., K.3, K.2 tog., w.f., K.2, rep. from + K.3.

8th row K.2, + P.5, K.3, P.4, rep. from + P.1, K.2.

9th & 37th rows K.2, + K.4, w.f., K.2 tog. t.b.l., K.1, K.2 tog., w.f., K.3, rep. from + K.3.

10th row K.2, + P.6, K.1, P.5, rep. from + P.1, K.2.

11th & 39th rows K.2, + K.5, w.f., sl.1, K.2 tog., p.s.s.o., w.f., K.4, rep. from + K.3.

12th row K.2, P. to last 2 sts., K.2.

13th, 15th, 17th, 19th, 21st, 23rd, 25th & 27th rows K.2, + K.2, w.f., K.2. tog. t.b.l., rep. from + K.3.

14th, 16th, 18th, 20th, 22nd, 24th, 26th & 28th rows K.2, P.1, + P.2, w.r.n., P.2 tog., rep. from + K.2.

30th row K.2, + K.1, P.11, rep. from + K.3.

32nd row K.2, + K.2, P.9, K.1, rep. from + K.3.

34th row K.2, + K.3, P.7, K.2, rep. from + K.3.

36th row K.2, + K.4, P.5, K.3, rep. from + K.3.

38th row K.2, + K.5, P.3, K.4, rep. from + K.3.

40th row K.2, + K.6, P.1, K.5, rep. from + K.3.

41st row K.2, + K.6, w.f., K.2 tog. t.b.l., K.4, rep. from + K.3.

42nd row K.2, P. to last 2 sts., K.2.

These 42 rows form the pattern

47

Madeira Leaf Pattern

Multiple of 12 + 5

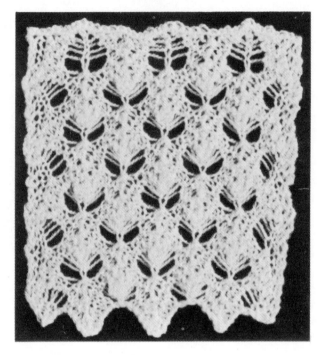

32

1st–6th rows K.2, + K.1, w.f., K.4, P.3 tog., K.4, w.f., rep. from + K.3.

7th–12th rows K.2, P.2 tog., + K.4, w.f., K.1, w.f., K.4, P.3 tog., rep. from + K.4, w.f., K.1, w.f., K.4, P.2 tog., K.2.

These 12 rows form the pattern

Diagonal Madeira Pattern

Multiple of 4 + 4

1st row K.2, + w.f., sl.1, K.2 tog., p.s.s.o., w.f., K.1, rep. from + K.2.

3rd row K.2, + K.1, w.f., sl.1, K.2 tog., p.s.s.o., w.f., rep. from + K.2.

2nd, 4th & 6th rows Purl.

48

33

5th row K.1, K.2 tog., + w.f., K.1, w.f., sl.1,
K.2 tog., p.s.s.o., rep. from + w.f., K.1, w.f.,
K.2 tog. t.b.l., K.2.

7th row K.2, K.2 tog., + w.f., K.1, w.f., sl.1,
K.2 tog., p.s.s.o., rep. from + w.f., K.1, w.f.,
K.2 tog. t.b.l., K.1.

8th row Purl.

These 8 rows form the pattern

Madeira Lace Edging Pattern

Cast on 37 sts.

1st row K.4, w.r.n., P.2 tog., K.4, w.f., K.5, w.f.,
K.1, w.f., K.5, (w.r.n., P.2 tog.) 7 times, w.o.n.,
K.2.

2nd row W.r.n., P.3 tog., (w.r.n., P.2 tog.)
8 times, K.1, p.2 tog., w.o.n., K.3, w.r.n., P.2
tog., K.1, P.2 tog., w.o.n., K.7, w.r.n., P.2 tog.,
K.2.

3rd row K.4, w.r.n., P.2 tog., K.6, P.3 tog.,
w.o.n., K.5, w.r.n., P.3 tog., (w.r.n., P.2 tog.)
8 times, K.1.

4th row W.r.n., P.3 tog., (w.r.n., P.2 tog.)
7 times, P.2 tog., w.r.n., P.2 tog., K.1, P.2 tog.,
w.o.n., K.10, w.r.n., P.2 tog., K.2.

5th row K.4, w.r.n., P.2 tog., K.5, P.2 tog., K.2,
w.r.n., P.3 tog., w.r.n., P.3 tog., (w.r.n., P.2
tog.) 7 times, K.1.

6th row W.r.n., P.3 tog., (w.r.n., P.2 tog.)
7 times, w.o.n., K.1, w.r.n., P.2 tog., K.9,
w.r.n., P.2 tog., K.2.

7th row K.4, w.r.n., P.2 tog., K.6, P.2 tog.,
w.o.n., K.3, (w.r.n., P.2 tog.) 7 times, w.o.n.,
K.2.

49

34

8th row (W.r.n., P.2 tog.) 8 times, w.o.n., K.5, w.r.n., P.2 tog., K.7, w.r.n., P.2 tog., K.2.

9th row K.4, w.r.n., P.2 tog., K.4, P.2 tog., w.o.n., K.1, w.r.n., P.2 tog., K.1, P.2 tog., w.o.n., K.1, (w.r.n., P.2 tog.) 7 times, w.o.n., K.2.

10th row (W.r.n., P.2 tog.) 8 times, w.o.n., K.3, w.r.n., P.3 tog., w.o.n., K.3, w.r.n., P.2 tog., K.5, w.r.n., P.2 tog., K.2.

These 10 rows form the pattern

III

Italian and French Knitting

WE HAVE no evidence as to the period at which Spanish Knitting moved from the sacred to the secular; that is when it ceased to be a craft carried on in the service of the Church and became one associated with the Secular fashions of the period. There seems to be no doubt, however, that the visits of Spanish nobles to Italy, particularly to Rome and Florence, were to have a decisive influence on Italian Knitting.

In Italy the craft became more self-conscious and more sophisticated. The designs lost something of their primitive origins and started to reflect the aesthetic movement that was to dominate Florence in particular, and was to reach its culmination in the Italian Renaissance.

We can still see outstanding examples of Italian fashion knitwear of the fifteenth and sixteenth centuries in the Florentine Coats and Jerkins that are to be found in many museums including the Victoria and Albert Museum in London. Here ornateness runs riot. Bright-coloured silk, silver and gold threads, even semi-precious stones are all at times used in the creation of floral and symbolic patternings that in many respects resembled the woven brocades of the same period.

It is also interesting to note that even in this later period of Italian knitting we still find traces of the Arabic influence in the self-coloured Dice and Diamond patterned designs that are found on the borders of most of these garments.

The Italians undoubtedly used hooked needles; in fact in common with the French, who use the word 'tricot' for either crochet or knitting, the same word is used in Italian for both crafts.

Although we can trace no historical continuity in the Italian story, the revival of Italian knitwear at the present time has placed them to the forefront of knitwear fashion. Even in our own age they are still using brocaded effects for some of the suits and dresses that form part of the *haute couture* of the Italian knitwear collections, and probably the influence of hooked knitting is still to be found in the crochet-knit fabrics that are tending more and more to dominate the Italian fashion story.

In France we find in the knitter's craft the marriage of the Spanish and Italian traditions. Spain had started to develop lace knitting as early as the twelfth century and we still find wonderful examples in Spanish lace, particularly in babies' wear, in Southern Spain at the present time.

The French specialised in the knitting of stockings whose elaborate lace patternings made them one of the marvels of Europe. Henry VIII had several pairs of French knitted hosiery and in Hatfield House you can still see in the museum there, a pair of lace stockings copied from a French design reputed to have been made by a Mrs. Montague, who was a Lady of the Chamber to Queen Elizabeth.

We can find little trace of colour knitting in France until just prior to the French Revolution, but today the tradition has been revived and we find Jacquard sweaters and jackets very popular in France at the present time.

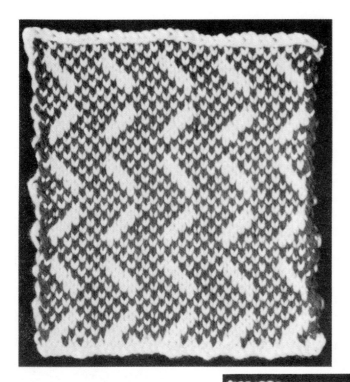

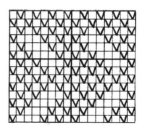

35

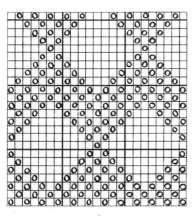

36

52

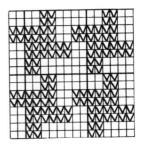

37

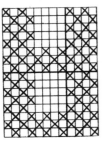

38

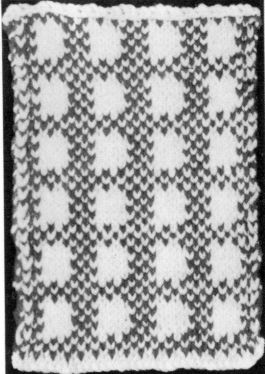

53

ITALIAN

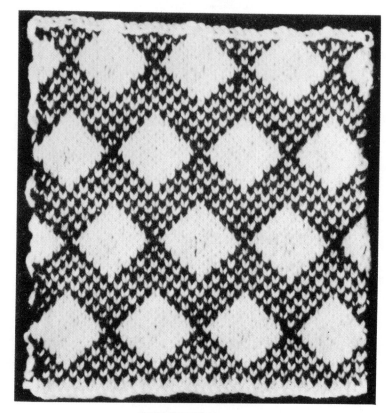

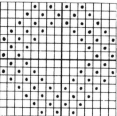

39

ITALIAN

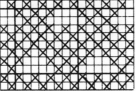

40

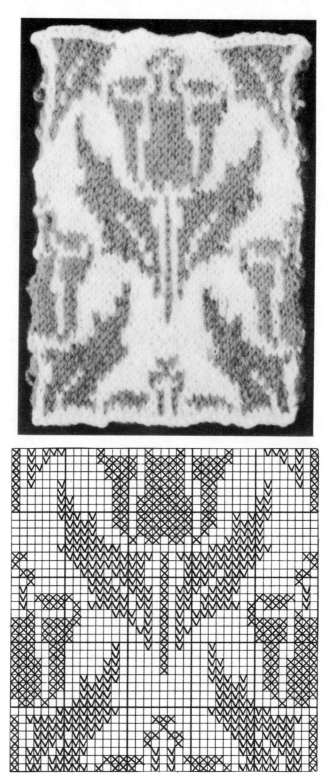

41

42

43

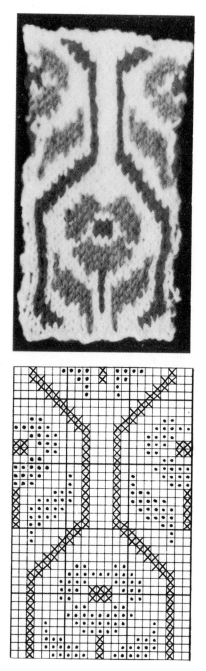

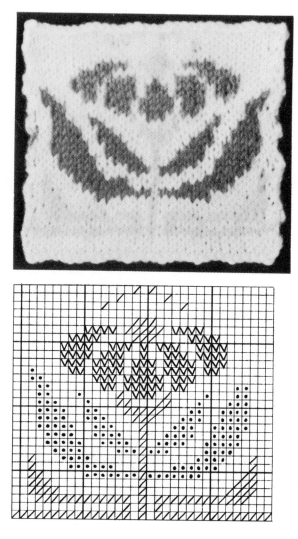

45

44

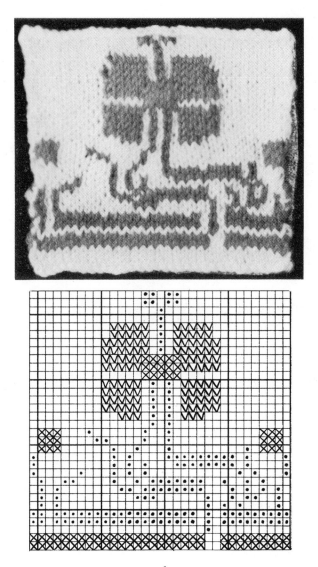

46

ITALIAN KNITTING PATTERNS

Crochet-knit Striped Pattern
Multiple of 6 + 2

47

1st row + K.1, P.1, K.2 tog., (w.f.) twice, K.2 tog. t.b.l., rep. from + K.1, P.1.

2nd row + P.1, K.1, P.1, P. into front of first w.f., P. into back of second w.f., P.1, rep. from + P.1, K.1.

3rd row + K.1, P.1, w.o.n., K.2 tog. t.b.l., K.2 tog., w.f., rep from + K.1, P.1.

4th row + P.1, K.1, P.4, rep. from + P.1, K.1.

These 4 rows form the pattern

Crochet-knit Ric-rac Pattern
Multiple of 3 + 1

1st row + K.B.1, M.1K, K.2 tog. t.b.l., rep. from + K.B.1.

2nd row +P.B.1, P.2, rep. from + P.B.1.

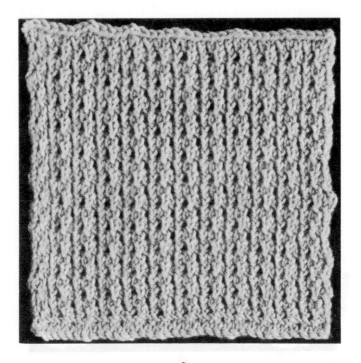

48

3rd row + K.B.1, K.2 tog., M.1K, rep. from + K.B.1.

4th row As 2nd.

These 4 rows form the pattern

Crochet-knit Travelling Eyelet Pattern
Multiple of 6 + 8

1st row K.1, w.f., K.2 tog. t.b.l., K.2, + K.2 tog., w.f., K.2 tog. t.b.l., K.2, rep. from + K.2 tog., w.f., K.1.

2nd row K.1, P.1, + P.4, P. into front and back of next st. (w.f. of previous row), rep. from + P.5, K.1.

49

3rd row K.2, + K.2 tog., w.f., K.2 tog. t.b.l., K.2, rep. from + to end.

4th row K.1, P.2, + P. into front and back of next st., P.4, rep. from + P. into front and back of next st., P.2, K.1.

These 4 rows form the pattern

Crochet-knit Shell Pattern

Multiple of 6 + 3

1st row K.1, + w.f., K.1, rep. from + K.1. (Wrong side.)

2nd row K. dropping w.f's of previous row.

3rd row K.1, K.3 tog., + (w.f.) twice, K1, (w.f.) twice, sl.2, K.3 tog., p.2.s.s.o., rep. from + (w.f.) twice, K.1, (w.f.) twice, K.3 tog., K.1.

4th row K.1, + K.1, (K. into front and back of 2 w.f's), rep. from + K.2.

5th & 6th rows As 1st & 2nd.

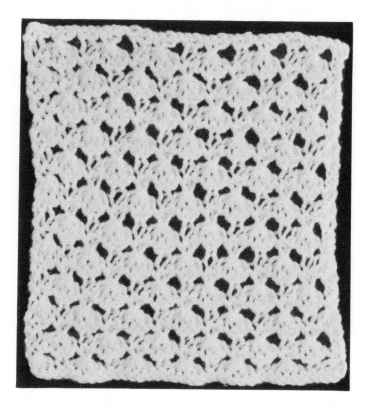

50

7th row K.1, + K.1, (w.f.) twice, sl.2, K.3 tog., p.2.s.s.o., (w.f.) twice, rep. from + K.2.

8th row As 4th.

These 8 rows form the pattern

Double Ric-rac Pattern (see page 64)

Multiple of 11 + 3

1st row K.1, + K.B.2, P.1, Tw.2F., Cr.2 by K.2 tog., then K. into 2nd st. before dropping st. off needle, Tw.2B, P.1, K.B.1, rep. from + K.B.1, K.1.

2nd row K.1, + P.B.2, K.1, P.6, K.1, P.B.1, rep. from + P.B.1, K.1.

3rd row K.1, + K.B.1, P.2, Tw.2B, Cr.2, Tw.2F., P.2, rep. from + K.B.1., K.1.

4th row K.1, + P.B.1, K.2, P.6, K.2, rep. from + P.B.1, K.1.

These 4 rows form the pattern

Crochet-knit Ladder Stitch Pattern

Multiple of 7 + 6

51

52

1st row K.1, + K.2 tog., (w.f.) twice, K.2 tog. t.b.l., K.3, rep. from + K.2 tog., (w.f.) twice, K.2 tog. t.b.l., K.1.

2nd row K.1, + K.1, (K.B.1, K.1) into w.f's of previous row, K.1, P.3, rep. from + K.1, (K.B.1, K.1), K.2.

3rd row K.1, + K.2 tog., (w.f.) twice, K.2 tog. t.b.l., Tw.3, rep. from + K.2 tog., (w.f.) twice, K.2 tog. t.b.l., K.1.

4th row K.1, + K.1, (K.B.1, K.1) into w.f's of previous row, K.1, P.3, rep. from + K.1, (K.B.1, K.1), K.2.

These 4 rows form the pattern

Lace Butterfly Pattern
Multiple of 14 + 4

1st row + P.1, Tw.2, P.1, K.3, K.2 tog., (w.f.) twice, K.2 tog. t.b.l., K.3, rep. from + P.1, Tw.2, P.1.

2nd row + K.1, P.2, K.1, P.4, (K.B.1, K.1, into w.f's), P.4, rep. from + K1, P.2, K.1.

3rd & 4th rows As 1st & 2nd.

5th row + P.1, Tw.2, P.1, K.1, K.2 tog., (w.f.) twice, K.2 tog. t.b.l., K.2 tog., (w.f.) twice, K.2 tog. t.b.l., K.1, rep. from + P.1, Tw.2, P.1.

6th row + K.1, P.2, K.1, P.2, (K.B.1, K.1), P.2, (K.B.1, K.1.), P.2, rep. from + K.1, P.2, K.1.

7th & 8th rows As 5th & 6th.

These 8 rows form the pattern

Miniature Leaf Pattern

Multiple of 6 + 3

54

1st row K.1, + K.1, w.f., K.2 tog. t.b.l., K.1, K.2 tog., w.f., rep. from + K.2.

2nd row K.1, + P.2, w.r.n., P.3 tog., w.r.n., P.1, rep. from + P.1, K.1.

3rd row Knit.

4th row K.1, + P.1, P.2 tog. t.b.l., w.r.n., P.1, w.r.n., P.2 tog., rep. from + P.1, K.1.

5th row K.1, K.2 tog., + w.f., K.3, w.f., K.3 tog., rep. from + w.f., K.3, w.f., K.2 tog. t.b.l., K.1.

6th row Purl.

These 6 rows form the pattern

Crochet-knit Treble Shell Pattern

Multiple of 4 + 2

55

1st row Purl. (Wrong side.)

2nd row K.1, + w.f., K.1, rep. from + K.1.

3rd row K.1, P. to last st., dropping w.f., of previous row, K.1.

4th row K.1, + work treble as follows: K. into 4th & 3rd sts., leave on needle, K. 1st st., drop off needle, K.1, drop all 3 sts. off needle, rep. from + K.1.

5th–7th rows As 1st–3rd.

8th row K.3, + work treble, rep. from + K.3.

These 8 rows form the pattern

Crochet-knit Trellis Pattern

Multiple of 4 + 2

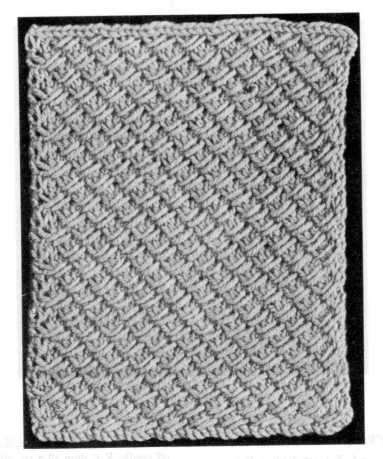

56

1st row (Wrong side) K.1, + P. to last st., wrapping wool twice round needle for each st., K.1.

2nd row K.1, + sl. next 4 sts. on to right-hand needle thus forming long sts; now sl. back on to left-hand needle; place point of right-hand needle *through* 3rd & 4th st. on left-hand needle, cross over 1st & 2nd st., then K.4 (this action is called Trellis Four), rep. from + K.1.

3rd row As 1st.

4th row K.3, + Trellis Four, rep. from + K.3.

These 4 rows form the pattern

Lace Vandyke Border Pattern

Multiple of 12 + 5

57

1st row   K.2, + K.1, w.f., K.2 tog. t.b.l., K.7, K.2 tog., w.f., rep from + K.3.

2nd row   K.2. + P.3, K.7, P.2, rep. from + P.1, K.2.

3rd row   K.2, + K.2, w.f., K.2 tog. t.b.l., K.5, K.2 tog., w.f., K.1, rep. from + K.3.

4th row   K.2, + P.4, K.5, P.3, rep. from + P.1, K.2.

5th row   K.2, + K.1, (w.f., K.2 tog. t.b.l.) twice, K.3, (K.2 tog., w.f.) twice, rep. from + K.3.

6th row   K.2, + P.5, K.3, P.4, rep. from + P.1, K.2.

7th & 11th rows   K.2, + K.2, (w.f., K.2 tog. t.b.l.) twice, K.1, (K.2 tog., w.f.) twice, K.1, rep. from + K.3.

8th row   K.2, + P.6, K.1, P.5, rep. from + P.1, K.2.

9th row   K.2, + K.1, (w.f., K.2 tog. t.b.l.) twice, w.f., sl.1, K.2 tog., p.s.s.o., w.f., (K.2 tog., w.f.) twice, rep. from + K.3.

10th row   K.2, + K.2, P.9, K.1, rep. from + K.3.

12th row   K.2, + K.3, P.7, K.2, rep. from + K.3.

13th row   K.2, + K.3, w.f., K.2 tog. t.b.l., w.f., sl.1, K.2 tog., p.s.s.o., w.f., K.2 tog., w.f., K.2, rep. from + K.3.

14th row   K.2, + K.4, P.5, K.3, rep. from + K.3.

15th row   K.2, + K.4, w.f., K.2 tog. t.b.l., K.1, K.2 tog., w.f., K.3, rep. from + K.3.

16th row   K.2, + K.5, P.3, K.4, rep. from + K.3.

17th row   K.2, + K.5, w.f., sl.1, K.2 tog., p.s.s.o., w.f., K.4, rep. from + K.3.

18th row   Knit.

These 18 rows form the pattern

Lace Medallion Pattern

Multiple of 11 + 4

58

1st row K.2, + K.3, K.2 tog., w.f., K.1, w.f., K.2 tog. t.b.l., K.3, rep. from + K.2.

2nd row K.2, + K.2, P.2 tog. t.b.l., w.r.n., P.3, w.r.n., P.2 tog., K.2, rep. from + K.2.

3rd row K.2, + K.1, (K.2 tog., w.f.) twice, K.1, (w.f., K.2 tog. t.b.l.) twice, K.1, rep. from + K.2.

4th row K.2, + P.2 tog. t.b.l., w.r.n., P.2 tog. t.b.l., w.o.n., K.3, (w.r.n., P. 2 tog.) twice, rep, from + K.2.

5th row K.2, + K.1, (w.f., K.2 tog. t.b.l.) twice, K.1, (K.2 tog., w.f.) twice, K.1, rep. from + K.2.

6th row K.2, + K.2, w.r.n., P.2 tog., w.r.n., P.3 tog., w.r.n., P.2 tog. t.b.l., w.o.n., K.2, rep. from + K.2.

7th row K.2, + K.3, w.f., K.2 tog. t.b.l., K.1, K.2 tog., w.f., K.3, rep. from + K.2.

8th row K.2, + K.4, w.r.n., P.3 tog., w.o.n., K.4, rep. from + K.2.

These 8 rows form the pattern

Wave and Leaf Pattern

Multiple of 10 + 5

1st row K.2, + w.f., K.2 tog. t.b.l., K.8, rep. from + w.f., K.2, tog. t.b.l., K.1.

2nd row K.2, + P.1, w.r.n., P.2 tog., P.5, P.2 tog., t.b.l., w.r.n., rep. from + P.1, K.2.

3rd row K.2, + K.2, w.f., K.2 tog. t.b.l., K.3, K.2 tog., w.f., K.1, rep. from + K.3.

4th row K.2, + P.3, w.r.n., P.2 tog., P.1, P.2 tog. t.b.l., w.r.n., P.2, rep. from + P.1, K.2.

5th row K.2, + K.4, w.f., sl.1, K.2 tog., p.s.s.o., w.f., K.3, rep. from + K.3.

6th & 22nd rows K.2, P. to last 2 sts., K.2.

7th row K.2, K.2 tog., + (w.f.) twice, K.2 tog. t.b.l., K.3, K.2 tog., (w.f.) twice, sl.1, K.2 tog., p.s.s.o., rep. from + (w.f.) twice, K.2 tog. t.b.l., K.3, K.2 tog., (w.f.) twice, K.2 tog. t.b.l., K.2.

8th, 14th, 26th & 28th rows K.2, + P.2, K.1, P.5, K.1, P.1, rep. from + P.1, K.2.

9th row K.2, + K.2, (w.f.) twice, sl.1, K.2 tog., p.s.s.o., K.1, K.3 tog., (w.f.) twice, K.1, rep. from + K.3.

59

10th, 12th, 24th & 30th rows K.2, + P.3, K.1, P.3, K.1, P.2, rep. from + P.1, K.2.

11th row K.2, + K.3, (w.f.) twice, sl.2, K.3 tog., p.2.s.s.o., (w.f.) twice, K.2, rep. from + K.3.

13th row K.2, + K.1, K.3 tog., (w.f.) twice, K.3, (w.f.) twice, sl.1, K.2 tog., p.s.s.o., rep. from + K.3.

15th row K.2, K.3 tog., + (w.f.) twice, K.5, (w.f.) twice, sl.2, K.3 tog., p.2.s.s.o., rep. from + (w.f.) twice, K.5, (w.f.) twice, sl.1, K.2 tog., p.s.s.o., K.2.

16th row K.2, + P.1, K.1, P.7, K.1, rep. from + P.1, K.2.

17th row K.2, + K.5, w.f., K.2 tog. t.b.l., K.3, rep. from + K.3.

18th row K.2, + P.3, P.2 tog. t.b.l., w.r.n., P.1, w.r.n., P.2 tog., P.2, rep. from + P.1, K.2.

19th row K.2, + K.2, K.2 tog., w.f., K.3, w.f., K.2 tog. t.b.l., K.1, rep from + K.3.

20th row K.2, + P.1, P.2 tog. t.b.l., w.r.n., P.5., w.r.n., P.2 tog., rep. from + P.1, K.2.

21st row K.2, K.2 tog., + w.f., K.7, w.f., sl.1, K.2 tog., p.s.s.o., rep. from + w.f., K.7, w.f., K.2 tog. t.b.l., K.2.

23rd row K.2, + K.2, K.2 tog., (w.f.) twice, sl.1, K.2 tog., p.s.s.o., (w.f.) twice, K.2 tog. t.b.l., K.1, rep. from + K.3.

25th row K.2, + K.1, K.3 tog., (w.f.) twice, K.3, (w.f.) twice, sl.1, K.2 tog., p.s.s.o., rep. from + K.3.

27th row K.2, K.3 tog., + (w.f.) twice, K.5, (w.f.) twice, sl.2, K.3 tog., p.2.s.s.o., rep. from + (w.f.) twice, K.5, (w.f.) twice, sl.1, K.2 tog., p.s.s.o., K.2.

29th row K.2, + K.2, (w.f.) twice, sl.1, K.2 tog., p.s.s.o., K.1, K.3 tog., (w.f.) twice, K.1, rep. from + K.3.

31st row K.2, + K.3, (w.f.) twice, sl.2, K.3 tog., p.2.s.s.o., (w.f.) twice, K.2, rep. from + K.3.

32nd row K.2, + P.4, K.1, P.1, K.1, P.3, rep. from + P.1, K.2.

These 32 rows form the pattern

Herringbone Pattern
Odd number of stitches

60

1st row (Wrong side) K.1, P. to last st., K.1.

2nd row K.2, + K.2 tog. t.b.l., K. into 2nd st., sl. sts. off needle, then sl. last st. back on to left-hand needle, rep. from + K.2.

3rd row K.1, P. to last st., K.1.

4th row K.1, + K.2 tog. t.b.l., K. into 2nd st. then sl. last st. back on to left-hand needle, rep. from + K.1.

These 4 rows form the pattern

Corded Rib Pattern

Multiple of 4 + 2

61

3rd row   + K.B.1, (P.1, K.1) 3 times, P.1, K.B.1,
P.2, K.4, rep. from + K.B.1, (P.1, K.1) 3 times,
P.1, K.B.1

They 4 every form the pattern

1st & every row   K.1, + K.2 tog. t.b.l., M.1K.,
P.2, rep. from + K.1.

Moss and Vandyke Pattern

Multiple of 15 + 9

1st row   + K.B.1, (P.1, K.1) 3 times, P.1, K.B.1,
K.4, P.2, rep. from + K.B.1, (P.1, K.1) 3 times,
P.1, K.B.1.

2nd row   + P.B.1, K.2, P.1, K.1, P.1, K.2,
P.B.1, P.1, K.2, P.3, rep. from + P.B.1, K.2,
P.1, K.1, P.1. K.2, P.B.1.

3rd row   + K.B.1, (P.1, K.1) 3 times, P.1, K.B.1,
K.2, P.2, K.2, rep. from + K.B.1, (P.1, K.1)
3 times, P.1, K.B.1.

4th row   + P.B.1, K.2, P.1, K.1, P.1, K.2, P.B.1,
P.3, K.2, P.1, rep. from + P.B.1, K.2, P.1,
K.1, P.1, K.2, P.B.1.

73

62

5th row   + K.B.1, (P.1, K.1) 3 times, P.1, K.B.1,   *6th row*   As 4th.
  P.2, K.4, rep. from + K.B.1, (P.1, K.1) 3 times,   *7th row*   As 3rd.
  P.1, K.B.1.   *8th row*   As 2nd.

These 8 rows form the pattern

Lozenge Pattern   (*see page 75*)

Multiple of 5

1st row   + P.1, K.4, rep. from +.   *6th & 7th rows*   + K.2, P.3, rep. from +.

2nd & 3rd rows   + P.3, K.2, rep. from +.   *8th row*   + K.4, P.1, rep. from +.

4th & 5th rows   + P.1, K.4, rep. from +.

These 8 rows form the pattern

74

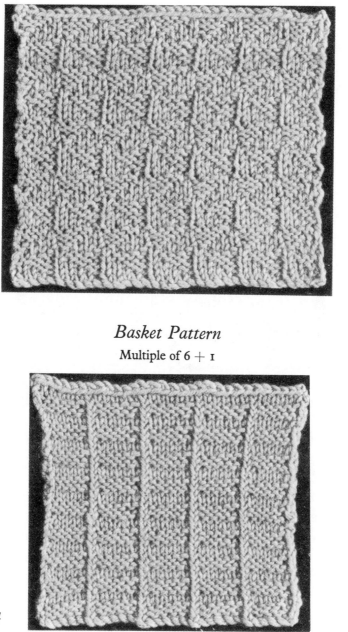

63

Basket Pattern

Multiple of 6 + 1

64

1st row + K.B.1, P.5, rep. from + K.B.1.	*3rd row* + K.B.1, K.5, rep. from + K.B.1.
2nd row + P.B.1, K.5, rep. from + P.B.1.	*4th row* + P.B.1, P.5, rep. from + P.B.1.

These 4 rows form the pattern

Zigzag Pattern
Multiple of 8

65

1st–4th rows + P.4, K.4, rep. from +.	*9th–12th rows* + K.4, P.4, rep. from +.
5th row + K.2, P.4, K.2, rep. from +.	*13th row* + P.2, K.4, P.2, rep. from +.
6th row + P.2, K.4, P.2, rep. from +.	*14th row* + K.2, P.4, K.2, rep. from +.
7th & 8th rows As 5th & 6th.	*15th & 16th rows* As 13th & 14th.

These 16 rows form the pattern

Embossed Rib Pattern
Multiple of 9 + 4

1st row + K.B.1, K.1, P.1, K.B.1, P.5, rep. from + K.B.1, K.1, P.1, K.B.1.

2nd row + P.B.1, K.1, P.1, P.B.1, K.5, rep. from + P.B.1, K.1, P.1, P.B.1.

76

66

3rd row + K.B.1, P.1, K.1, K.B.1, P.5, rep. from + K.B.1, P.1, K.1, K.B.1.

4th row + P.B.1, P.1, K.1, P.B.1, K.5, rep. from + P.B.1, P.1, K.1, P.B.1.

These 4 rows form the pattern

Embossed Ladder Pattern

Multiple of 14

1st row + K.B.1, P.2, K.B.1, P.1, K.2, P.2, K.1, K.B.1, P.2, K.B.1, rep. from +.

2nd row + (P.B.1, K.2) twice, P.2, (K.2, P.B.1) twice, rep. from +.

77

67

3rd row + K.B.1, P.2, K.B.1, K.1, P.2, K.2, P.1, K.B.1, P.2, K.B.1, rep. from +.

4th row + P.B.1, K.2, P.B.1, P.2, K.2, P.2, P.B.1, K.2, P.B.1, rep. from +.

These 4 rows form the pattern

Embossed Vandyke Pattern
Multiple of 8

1st row + K.B.4, P.4, rep. from +.

2nd row + K.4, P.B.4, rep. from +.

3rd row + P.1, K.B.4, P.3, rep. from +.

4th row + K.3, P.B.4, K.1, rep. from +.

5th row + P.2, K.B.4, P.2, rep. from +.

6th row + K.2, P.B.4, K.2, rep. from +.

7th row + P.3, K.B.4, P.1, rep. from +.

8th row + K.1, P.B.4, K.3, rep. from +.

9th row + P.4, K.B.4, rep. from +.

10th row + P.B.4, K.4, rep. from +.

68

11th row + K.B.1, P.4, K.B.3, rep. from +.	*14th row* + P.B.2, K.4, P.B.2, rep. from +.
12th row + P.B.3, K.4, P.B.1, rep. from +.	*15th row* + K.B.3, P.4, K.B.1, rep. from +.
13th row + K.B.2, P.4, K.B.2, rep. from +.	*16th row* + P.B.1, K.4, P.B.3, rep. from +.

These 16 rows form the pattern

Embossed Pyramid Pattern
Multiple of 8 + 1

1st row   + P.1, K.B.1, rep. from + P.1.

2nd row   + K.1, P.B.1, rep. from + K.1.

3rd & 4th rows   As 1st & 2nd.

5th row   + P.2, (K.B.1, P.1) 3 times, rep. from + P.1.

6th row   + K.2, (P.B.1, K.1) 3 times, rep. from + K.1.

7th & 8th rows   As 5th & 6th.

9th row   + P.3, K.B.1, P.1, K.B.1, P.2, rep. from + P.1.

10th row   + K.3, P.B.1, K.1, P.B.1, K.2, rep. from + K.1.

69

11th & 12th rows As 9th & 10th.	*14th row* + K.4, P.B.1, K.3, rep. from + K.1.
13th row + P.4, K.B.1, P.3, rep. from + P.1.	*15th & 16th rows* As 13th & 14th.

These 16 rows form the pattern

Embossed Chequer Pattern

Multiple of 2 + 1

1st row   K.B. all across.

2nd row   + K.1, P.B.1, rep. from + K.1.

3rd row   + P.1, K.B.1, rep. from + P.1.

4th row   As 2nd.

5th row   As 1st.

6th row   + P.B.1, K.1, rep. from + P.B.1.

7th row   + K.B.1, P.1, rep. from + K.B.1.

8th row   As 6th.

These 8 rows form the pattern

70

71

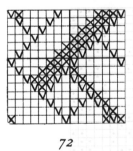

72

FRENCH

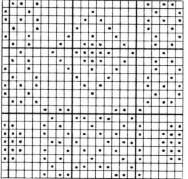

73

FRENCH

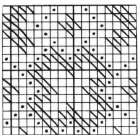

74

75

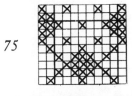

76

FRENCH KNITTING PATTERNS

Travelling Vine Pattern
Multiple of 8 + 4

77

1st row   K.2, + w.f., K.B.1, w.f., K.2 tog. t.b.l., K.5, rep. from + K.2.

2nd row   P.2, + P.4, P.2 tog. t.b.l., P.3, rep. from + P.2.

3rd row   K.2, + w.f., K.B.1, w.f., K.2, K.2 tog. t.b.l., K.3, rep. from + K.2.

4th row   P.2, + P.2, P.2 tog. t.b.l., P.5, rep. from + P.2.

5th row   K.2, + K.B.1, w.f., K.4, K.2 tog. t.b.l., K.1, w.f., rep. from + K.2.

6th row   P.2, + P. 1, P.2 tog. t.b.l., P.6, rep. from + P.2.

7th row   K.2, + K.5, K.2 tog., w.f., K.B.1, w.f., rep. from + K.2.

8th row   P.2, + P.3, P.2 tog., P.4, rep. from + P.2.

9th row K.2, + K.3, K.2 tog., K.2, w.f., K.B.1, w.f., rep. from + K.2.

10th row P.2, + P.5, P.2 tog., P.2, rep. from + P.2.

11th row K.2, + w.f., K.1, K.2 tog., K.4, w.f., K.B.1, rep. from + K.2.

12th row P.2, + P.6, P.2 tog., P.1, rep. from + P.2.

(Note that on all odd rows 1 st. extra is added and on even rows 1 st. is lost thus bringing the sts. back to the original number.)

These 12 rows form the pattern

Florette Pattern
Multiple of 6 + 5

78

1st row K.2, + K.1, w.f., K.2 tog. t.b.l., K.1, K.2 tog., w.f., rep. from + K.3.

2nd & every alt. row Purl.

3rd row K.2, + K.2, w.f., K.3, w.f., K.1, rep. from + K.3.

5th row K.2, K.2 tog., + w.f., K.2 tog. t.b.l., K.1, K.2 tog., w.f., sl.1, K.2 tog., p.s.s.o., rep. from + w.f., K.2 tog. t.b.l., K.1, K.2 tog., w.f., K.2 tog. t.b.l., K.2.

7th row K.2, + K.1, K.2 tog., w.f., K.1, w.f., K.2 tog. t.b.l., rep. from + K.3.

9th row K.2, + K.2, w.f., K.3, w.f., K.1, rep. from + K.3.

11th row K.2, + K.1, K.2 tog., w.f., sl.1, K.2 tog., p.s.s.o., w.f., K.2 tog. t.b.l., rep. from + K.3.

12th row Purl.

(Note that number of sts. are increased on 3rd and 9th rows and decreased back to their original number on the 5th and 11th rows).

These 12 rows form the pattern

Travelling Eyelet Pattern
Multiple of 7 + 6

79

1st, 3rd & 5th rows K.2, + P.2, w.o.n., K.2 tog. t.b.l., K.1, K.2 tog., w.r.n., rep. from + P.2, K.2

2nd, 4th, 6th, 8th, 10th, 12th & 14th rows K.2, + K.2, P.5, rep. from + K.4.

86

7th & 15th rows K.2, + P.2, K.5, rep. from + P.2, K.2.

9th, 11th & 13th rows K.2, + P.2, K.2 tog., w.f. K.1, w.f., K.2 tog. t.b.l., rep. from + P.2, K.2.

16th row K.2, + K.2, P.5, rep. from + K.4.

These 16 rows form the pattern

Travelling Leaf Pattern
Multiple of 16 + 5

80

1st & 3rd rows K.2, + K.1, w.f., K.5, K.2 tog., K.1, K.2 tog. t.b.l., K.5, w.f., rep. from + K.3.

2nd, 4th & 6th rows Purl.

5th & 7th rows K.2, + K.1, K.2 tog. t.b.l., K.5, w.f., K.1, w.f., K.5, K.2 tog., rep. from + K.3.

8th row Purl.

These 8 rows form the pattern

87

Multiple of 12 + 5

81

1st & 7th rows   K.2, + K.4, P.2 tog., w.o.n., K.1, w.r.n., P.2 tog., K.3, rep. from + K.3.

2nd & every alt. row   Purl.

3rd & 5th rows   K.2, + K.4, w.r.n., P.2 tog., K.1, P.2 tog., w.o.n., K.3, rep. from + K.3.

9th & 15th rows   K.2, + K.1, w.r.n., P.2 tog., K.7, P.2 tog., w.o.n., rep. from + K.3.

11th & 13th rows   K.2, + K.1, P.2 tog., w.o.n., K.7, w.r.n., P.2 tog., rep. from + K.3.

16th row   Purl.

These 16 rows form the pattern

Shower Stitch Pattern
Multiple of 12 + 4

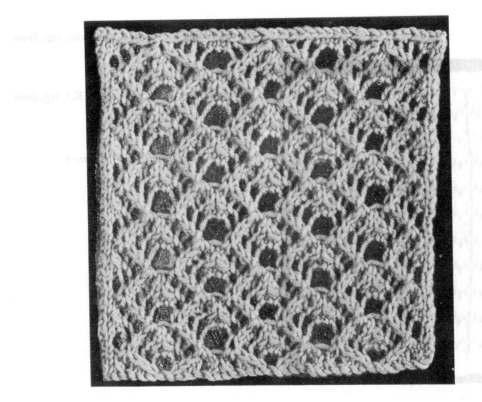

82

1st row K.2, + K.2 tog., w.f., K.2, K.2 tog., (w.f.) twice, K.2 tog. t.b.l., K.2, w.f., K.2 tog. t.b.l., rep. from + K.2.

2nd row P.2, + P.3, P.2 tog. t.b.l., w.o.n., (K.1, P.1, into 2 w.f's of previous row) w.r.n., P.2 tog., P.3, rep. from + P.2.

3rd row K.2, + K.2, K.2 tog., w.f., K.4, w.f., K.2 tog. t.b.l., K.2, rep. from + K.2.

4th row P.2, + P.3 tog. t.b.l., w.r.n., P.1, w.r.n., P.4, w.r.n., P.1, w.r.n., P.3 tog., rep. from + P.2.

5th row K.2, + w.f., K.2 tog. t.b.l., K.2, w.f., K.2 tog. t.b.l., K.2 tog., w.f., K.2, K.2 tog., w.f., rep. from + K.2.

6th row P.2, + P.1, w.r.n., P.2 tog., P.6, P.2 tog. t.b.l., w.o.n., K.1, rep. from + P.2.

7th row K.2, + K.2, w.f., K.2 tog. t.b.l., (K.1, K.2 tog.) twice, w.f., K.2, rep. from + K.2.

8th row P.2, + P.2, w.r.n., P.1, w.r.n., P.3 tog., P.2 tog. t.b.l., w.r.n., P.1, w.r.n., P.2, rep. from + P.2.

These 8 rows form the pattern

Honeycomb Tweed Pattern

Odd number of stitches

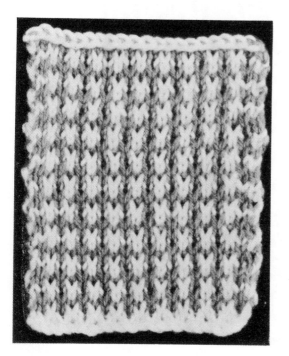

1st row Using L: + K.1, sl.1 purlwise, rep. from + K.1.

2nd row Using L: Purl.

3rd row Using D: K.2, + sl.1P., K.1, rep. from + K.1.

4th row Using D: Purl.

These 4 rows form the pattern

83

Striped Check Pattern *(see page 91)*

Multiple of 4 + 3

1st row Using 1st C: K.1, + sl.1 purlwise, K.3, rep. from + sl.1P., K.1.

2nd row Using 1st C: P.1, + keeping wool at front, sl.1P., P.3, rep. from + sl.1P., P.1.

3rd row Using 2nd C: K.3, + sl.1P., K3, rep. from + to end.

4th row Using 2nd C: P.3, + keeping wool at back, sl.1P., P.3, rep. from + to end.

5th & 6th rows Using 3rd C: As 1st & 2nd.

7th & 8th rows Using 4th C: As 3rd & 4th.

These 8 rows form the pattern

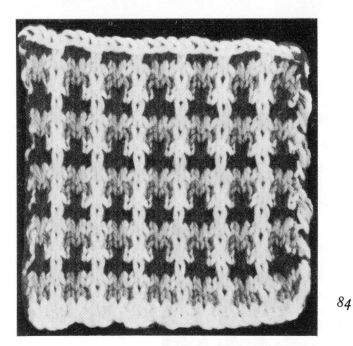

84

Tweed Knot Stitch Pattern

Odd number of stitches

85

1st row (Wrong side.) Using D: Knit.

2nd row Using D: + K.1, K. into loop below next st. and drop st. off needle, rep. from + K.1.

3rd row Using L: Knit.

4th row Using L: K.2, + K. into loop below, K.1, rep. from + K.1.

These 4 rows form the pattern

Bubble Tweed Pattern

Multiple of 3 + 2

1st row Using L: K.1, + sl.1 purlwise, K.2 tog. t.b.l., M.1K., rep. from + K.1.

2nd row Using L: P.1, + P.2, keeping wool at front sl.1P., rep. from + P.1.

3rd row Using D: K.2, + sl.1P., K.2 tog. t.b.l., M.1K., rep. from + sl.1, K.2.

4th row Using D: P.2, + sl.1P., keeping wool at front P.2, rep. from + to end.

5th row Using L: K.3, + sl.1P., K.2 tog. t.b.l., M.1K., rep. from + sl.1, K.1.

6th row Using L: P.1, + keeping wool at front sl.1P., P.2, rep. from + P.1.

7th & 8th rows Using D: As 1st & 2nd.

9th & 10th rows Using L: As 3rd & 4th.

11th & 12th rows Using D: As 5th & 6th.

86

These 12 rows form the pattern

Stripe and Spot Pattern

Odd number of stitches

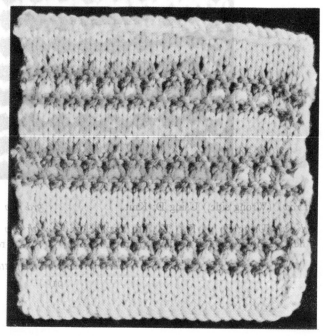

1st row Using L: Knit.

2nd row Using L: Purl.

3rd & 4th rows As 1st & 2nd.

5th & 6th rows Using M: Knit.

87

7th row   Using 1st C: + K.1, sl.1 purlwise, rep. from + K.1.

8th row   Using 1st C: + K.1, w.f., sl.1P., w.b., rep. from + K.1. Break off 1st C.

9th & 10th rows   Using M: Knit.

11th row   Using L: K.1, + K.1, sl.1P., rep. from + K.2.

12th row   Using L: P.2, + keeping wool at front sl.1P., P.1, rep. from + P.1.

13th–18th rows   As 1st–6th.

19th row   Using 2nd C: K.2, + sl.1P., K.1, rep. from + K.1.

20th row   Using 2nd C: K.2, + w.f., sl.1P., w.b., K.1, rep. from + K.1.

21st & 22nd rows   As 9th & 10th.

23rd row   Using L: + K.1, sl.1P., rep. from + K.1.

24th row   Using L: + P.1, keeping wool at front sl.1P., rep. from + P.1.

These 24 rows form the pattern

Twisted Ladder Pattern
Multiple of 5 + 4

1st row   Using G: K.1, + Tw.2, K.3, rep. from + Tw.2, K.1.

2nd row   Using G: K.1, + P.2, K.3, rep. from + P.2, K.1.

3rd row   Using C: K.1, + sl.2 purlwise, K.3, rep. from + sl.2P., K.1.

4th row   Using C: K.1, + w.f., sl.2P., w.b., K.3, rep. from + w.f., sl.2P., w.b., K.1.

These 4 rows form the pattern

88

Honeycomb Trellis Pattern
Multiple of 12 + 2

1st row   K.1, + P.4, Cr.1F., Cr.1B., P.4, rep. from + K.1.

2nd row   K.1, + K.4, P.4, K.4, rep. from + K.1.

3rd row   K.1, + P.4, Cr.1B., Cr.1F., P.4, rep. from + K.1.

4th row   As 2nd.

5th–8th rows   Rep. 1–4.

9th row   K.1, + P.3, Tr.1B., Tr.2F., P.3, rep. from + K.1.

10th row   K.1, + K.3, P.2, K.2, P.2, K.3, rep. from + K.1.

11th row   K.1, + P.2, Tr.1B., P.2, Tr.2F., P.2, rep. from + K.1.

12th row   K.1, + K.2, P.2, K.4, P.2, K.2, rep. from + K.1.

89

13th row   K.1, + P.1, Tr.1B., P.4, Tr.2F., P.1, rep. from + K.1.

14th row   K.1, + K.1, P.2, K.6, P.2, K.1, rep. from + K.1.

15th row   K.1, + Tr.1B., P.6, Tr.2F., rep. from + K.1.

16th row   K.1, + P.2, K.8, P.2, rep. from + K.1.

17th row   K.3, P.8, + C.2F., P.8, rep. from + K.3.

18th row   As 16th.

19th row   K.1, + Tr.2F., P.6, Tr.1B., rep. from + K.1.

20th row   As 14th.

21st row   K.1, + P.1, Tr.2F., P.4, Tr.1B., P.1, rep. from + K.1.

22nd row   As 12th.

23rd row   K.1, + P.2, Tr.2F., P.2, Tr.1B., P.2, rep. from + K.1.

24th row   As 10th.

25th row   K.1, + P.3, Tr.2F., Tr.1B., P.3, rep. from + K.1.

26th row   K.1, + K.4, P.4, K.4, rep. from + K.1.

These 26 rows form the pattern

Tulip Pattern

Multiple of 3

90

1st row + K.B.1, K.2, rep. from +.

2nd row + P.2, P.B.1, rep. from +.

3rd & 4th rows As 1st & 2nd.

5th row + K.B.1, P.1, K.B.1, rep. from +.

6th row + P.B.1, K.1, P.B.1, rep. from +.

7th & 8th rows As 5th & 6th.

9th row + P.2, K.B.1, rep. from +.

10th row + P.B.1, K.2, rep. from +.

11th & 12th rows As 9th & 10th.

These 12 rows form the pattern

Chain Cable Pattern

Multiple of 11 + 7

1st row + P.7, C.B.2B., rep. from + P.7.

2nd row + (K.1, P.1) 3 times, K.1, P.B.4, rep. from + (K.1, P.1) 3 times, K.1.

3rd row + (P.1, w.o.n., sl.1 purlwise) 3 times, P.1., K.B.4, rep. from + (P.1, w.o.n., sl.1P.) 3 times, P.1.

4th row + (K.1, w.f., sl.1P., dropping w.o.n. of previous row, w.b.) 3 times, K.1, P.B.4, rep. from + (K.1, w.f., sl.1P. as before, w.b.) 3 times, K.1.

95

91

5th row + (P.1, keeping wool at back sl.1P.) 3 times, P.1, K.B.4, rep. from + (P.1, keeping wool at back sl.1P.) 3 times, P.1.

6th row + (K.1, w.f., sl.1P., w.b.) 3 times, K.1, P.B.4, rep. from + (K.1, w.f., sl.1P., w.b.) 3 times, K.1.

These 6 rows form the pattern

Figure of Eight Pattern (see page 97)

Multiple of 9 + 2

1st row + K.2, P.2, Tw.3, P.2, rep. from + K.2.

2nd row + P.2, K.2, P.3, K.2, rep. from + P.2.

3rd row + P.4, Tw.3, P.2, rep. from + P.2.

4th row As 2nd.

5th–8th rows Rep. 1–4 once more.

9th & 10th rows As 1st & 2nd.

11th row + P.4, K.3, P.2, rep. from + P.2.

12th row As 2nd.

13th–16th rows As 9th–12th.

These 16 rows form the pattern

92

Ear of Corn Pattern (see page 98)

Multiple of 11 + 4

1st row Using M: + Cr.1F., Cr.1B., K.7, rep. from + Cr.1F., Cr.1B.

2nd row Purl.

3rd row + Cr.1F., Cr.1B., P.1, K.6, rep. from + Cr.1F., Cr.1B.

4th row + P.9, K.2, rep. from + P.4.

5th row + Cr.1F., Cr.1B., P.3, K.4, rep. from + Cr.1F., Cr.1B.

6th row + P.7, K.4, rep. from + P.4.

7th row + Cr.1F., Cr.1B., P.5, K.2, rep. from + Cr.1F., Cr.1B.

8th row + P.5, K.6, rep. from + P.4.

9th–16th rows Using C: Rep. 1–8.

These 16 rows form the pattern

97

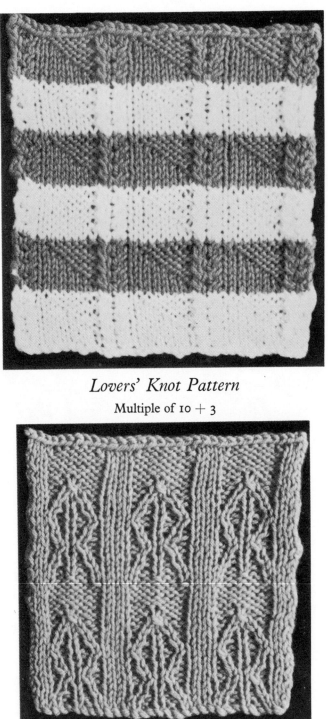

93

Lovers' Knot Pattern

Multiple of 10 + 3

94

1st row + K.4, P.2, K.1, P.2, K.1, rep. from + K.3.

2nd row + P.4, K.2, P.1, K.2, P.1, rep. from + P.3.

3rd row + K.3, sl.1F., P.1., K.1, P.1, sl.1B., rep. from + K.3.

4th row + P.3, (K.1, P.1) 3 times, K.1, rep. from + P.3.

5th row + K.3, P.1, sl.1F., K.1, sl.1B., P.1, rep. from + K.3.

6th row + (P.3, K.2) twice, rep. from + P.3.

7th row + K.3, P.1, sl.1B., K.1, sl.1F., P.1, rep. from + K.3.

8th row As 4th.

9th row + K.3, sl.1B., P.1, K.1, P.1, sl.1F., rep. from + K.3.

10th row As 2nd.

11th–14th rows As 3rd–6th.

15th row + K.3, P.2, M.1P., w.b., sl.1, K.2 tog., p.s.s.o., M.1P., P.2, rep. from + K.3.

16th row + P.3, K.7, rep. from + P.3.

17th row + K.3, P.7, rep. from + K.3.

18th row As 16th.

19th row As 17th.

20th row + P.4, K.5, P.1, rep. from + P.3.

These 20 rows form the pattern

99

IV

German and Austrian knitting

TRADITIONAL KNITTING PATTERNS in Germany and Austria illustrate to perfection a different phase in the development of the craft from those we have seen in the earlier chapters of this book. We must remember that today we see Germany and Austria as two large countries almost covering the centre of the European Continent.

It is interesting to remember that prior to the twentieth century both these countries had quite a different geographical background to the one we know today. The unification of the Austro-German Empire had certainly welded together the group of states that formed these two countries, but had not been able to stamp out the local traditions and regional habits that one still finds in both these countries.

Pause for a moment to consider that in southern Austria the local *patois* is sprinkled with Italian phrases; as one moves eastward one discovers the southern language; that again is distinct from German although both German and Austrian have a common derivation, is definitely influenced by Russian; move westwards where Germany borders on France and you will discover border towns and villages where both languages are spoken quite fluently.

It is only when we recognise these regional developments that took place in middle Europe from the ninth century onwards, that we can understand the wide diversity to be found in the knitting patterns common and local to these areas.

The gaiety of Vienna is captured in the cobweb-like lace for which she is world-famous. The knitting of this was taught originally in the convents, but today in the art schools in Vienna there are special classes that have maintained and preserved this ancient legacy. Move into the Austrian Tyrol and there you have the rural robustness of a Morris Dance. The patterns themselves are simple shapes copying leaves and flowers, the fabric itself being liberally sprinkled with touches of light coloured embroidery reminiscent of the floral splendour of the mountainsides of the Tyrol in late spring.

Pause for a moment to think of the Bavarian influence. Here in the heavy wooded forests that surround towns and villages, that were completely isolated from the rest of the community until means of modern transport were available, we find heavy fabrics full of cables, twists and knots reminiscent of the gnarled branches of the old trees that can still be seen in woodland places.

North Germany tells still a different story. Here the influence of the Puritan Revolt that swept Europe during the Reformation, has left a mark of austerity on knitted fabrics. They are as simple and as delightful as the quaint customs of the early Quakers who witnessed to simplicity in their way of life and the clothes they wore.

Even today we find this diversity has been preserved and modern means of communication, the moving of peoples from one section of Germany and Austria to another, the influence of industrial developments in both countries, have all to a certain extent unified the approach to the knitter's craft. The regional influences are still very strong.

You can still buy a knitted peasant-coat in the villages of the Tyrol, the pattern of which can be traced back for at least two or three hundred years. You can still see the exquisite laces in Vienna that graced the tables and probably the underclothes of the Court of Maria Theresa. You can still buy in the village shops in Bavaria, heavy jerseys the patterning on which is again at least a hundred to a hundred and fifty years old. No matter how much modern developments may destroy regional boundaries, regional customs and traditions are still well preserved.

95

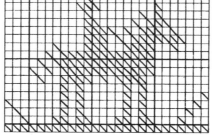

96

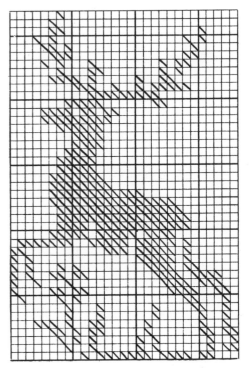

97

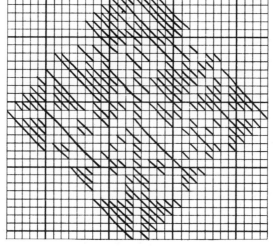

98

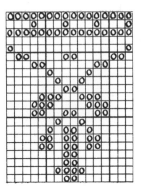

99

100

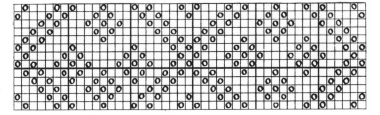

GERMAN

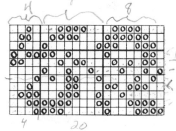

101

102

103

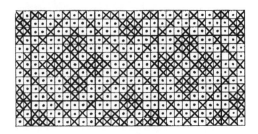

104

GERMAN

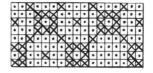

105

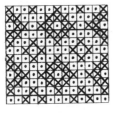

106

Bell Rib Pattern
Multiple of 11 + 6

107

1st row   (Wrong side) + K.2, P.2, K.2, P.5, rep. from + K.2, P.2, K.2.

2nd row   + P.2, Tw.2, P.2, w.o.n., K.2 tog. t.b.l., K.1, K.2 tog., w.r.n., rep. from + P.2, Tw.2, P.2.

3rd row   + K.2, P.2, K.3, P.3, K.1, rep. from + K.2, P.2, K.2.

4th row   + P.2, Tw.2, P.3, K.3, P.1, rep. from + P.2, Tw.2, P.2.

5th row   + K.2, P.2, K.3, w.r.n., P.3 tog., w.o.n., K.1, rep. from + K.2, P.2, K.2.

6th row   + P.2, Tw.2, P.4, K.1, P.2, rep. from + P.2, Tw.2, P.2.

These 6 rows form the pattern

Ribbed Beehive Pattern
Multiple of 6 + 3

1st row (Wrong side) K.1, + P.B.1, K.1, P.3, K.1, rep. from + P.B.1, K.1.

2nd row K.1, + K.B.1, P.1, w.o.n., sl.1, K.2 tog., p.s.s.o., w.r.n., P.1, rep. from + K.B.1, K.1.

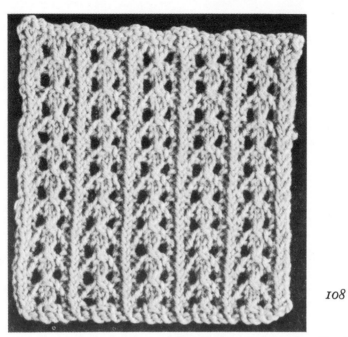

108

3rd row As 1st.

4th row K.1, + K.B.1, P.1, K.3, P.1, rep. from + K.B.1, K.1.

These 4 rows form the pattern

Trellis Ladder Pattern

Multiple of 12 + 3

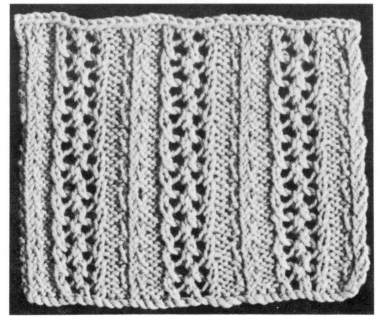

109

1st row K.1, + K.B.1, P.3, K.1, (w.f., K.2 tog. t.b.l.) twice, P.3, rep. from + K.B.1, K.1.

2nd row K.1, + P.B.1, K.3, P.5, K.3, rep. from + P.B.1, K.1.

3rd row K.1, + K.B.2, P.2, (K.2 tog., w.f.) twice, K.1, P.2, K.B.1, rep. from + K.B.1, K.1.

4th row K.1, + P.B.2, K.2, P.5, K.2, P.B.1, rep. from + P.B.1, K.1.

These 4 rows form the pattern

Waffle Rib Pattern
Multiple of 10 + 3

110

1st row K.1, + K.B.1, K.1, P.2, w.o.n., K.2 tog. t.b.l., K.1, P.2, K.1, rep. from + K.B.1, K.1.

2nd row K.1, + P.B.1, K.3, P.3, K.3, rep. from + P.B.1, K.1.

3rd row K.1, + K.B.1, K.1, P.2, K.1, K.2 tog., w.r.n., P.2, K.1, rep. from + K.B.1, K.1.

4th row K.1, + P.B.1, K.3, P.3, K.3, rep. from + P.B.1, K.1.

These 4 rows form the pattern

Clustered Cable Pattern
Multiple of 12 + 6

1st row + P.6, K.3, K.B.3, rep. from + P.6.

2nd row + K.6, P.B.3, P.3, rep. from + K.6.

3rd & 4th rows As 1st & 2nd.

5th row + P.6, sl. next 3 sts. on cable needle, leave at back, K.B.3, then K.3 across sts. on cable needle, rep. from + P.6.

6th row + K.6, P.3, P.B.3, rep. from + K.6.

III

7th row + K.3, K.B.3, P.6, rep. from + K.3, K.B.3.

8th row + P.B.3, P.3, K.6, rep. from + P.B.3, P.3.

9th & 10th rows As 7th & 8th.

11th row + C.3, as on 5th row, P.6, rep. from + C.3.

12th row + P.3, P.B.3, K.6, rep. from + P.3, P.B.3.

These 12 rows form the pattern

Travelling Cable Pattern

Multiple of 5 + 1

1st row + P.1, K.B.4, rep. from + P.1.

2nd row + K.1, P.B.4, rep. from + K.1.

3rd & 4th rows As 1st & 2nd.

5th row + P.1, CB.2F., rep. from + P.1.

6th row As 2nd.

7th row K.B.1, + P.1, K.B.4, rep. from +.

8th row + P.B.4, K.1, rep. from + P.B.1.

9th & 10th rows As 7th & 8th.

11th row K.B.1, + P.1, CB.2F., rep. from +.

12th row As 8th.

13th row K.B.2, + P.1, K.B.4, rep. from + P.1, K.B.3.

14th row P.B.3, + K.1, P.B.4, rep. from + K.1, P.B.2.

15th & 16th rows As 13th & 14th.

17th row K.B.2, + P.1, CB.2F., rep. from + P.1, K.B.3.

112

18th row   As 14th.

19th row   K.B.3, + P.1, K.B.4, rep. from + P.1, K.B.2.

20th row   P.B.2, + K.1, P.B.4, rep. from + K.1, P.B.3.

21st & 22nd rows   As 19th & 20th.

23rd row   K.B.3, + P.1, CB.2F., rep. from + P.1, K.B.2.

24th row   As 20th.

25th row   + K.B.4, P.1, rep. from + K.B.1.

26th row   P.B.1, + K.1, P.B.4, rep. from +.

27th & 28th rows   As 25th & 26th.

29th row   + CB.2F., P.1, rep. from + P.1, K.B.1.

30th row   P.B.1, + K.1, P.B.4, rep. from +.

These 30 rows form the pattern

Fuchsia Pattern
Multiple of 8

113

1st row	+ P.3, K.2, w.r.n., P.3, rep. from +.
2nd row	+ K.3, P.3, K.3, rep. from +.
3rd row	+ P.3, K.3, w.r.n., P.3, rep. from +.
4th row	+ K.3, P.4, K.3, rep. from +.
5th row	+ P.3, K.4, w.r.n., P.3, rep. from +.
6th row	+ K.3, P.5, K.3, rep. from +.
7th row	+ P.3, K.3, K.2 tog., P.3, rep. from +.
8th row	+ K.3, P.4, K.3, rep. from +.
9th row	+ P.3, K.2, K.2 tog., P.3, rep. from +.
10th row	+ K.3, P.3, K.3, rep. from +.
11th row	+ P.3, K.1, K.2 tog., P.3, rep. from +.
12th row	+ K.3, P.2, K.3, rep. from +.

These 12 rows form the pattern

Embossed Leaf Pattern (1)
Multiple of 8 + 1

1st row	+ P.4, K.1, w.r.n., P.3, rep. from + P.1.
2nd row	+ K.4, P.2, K.3, rep. from + K.1.
3rd row	+ P.4, K.2, w.r.n., P.3, rep. from + P.1.
4th row	+ K.4, P.3, K.3, rep. from + K.1.
5th row	+ P.4, K.3, w.r.n., P.3, rep. from + P.1.
6th row	+ K.4, P.4, K.3, rep. from + K.1.
7th row	+ P.4, K.4, P.3, rep. from + P.1.
8th row	As 6th.
9th row	+ P.4, K.2, K.2 tog., P.3, rep. from + P.1.
10th row	+ K.4, P.3, K.3, rep. from + K.1.
11th row	+ P.4, K.1, K.2 tog., P.3, rep. from + P.1.
12th row	+ K.4, P.2, K.3, rep. from + K.1.
13th row	+ P.4, K.2 tog., P.3, rep. from + P.1.
14th row	+ K.4, P.1, K.3, rep. from + K.1.

15th row	Purl.
16th row	Knit.

These 16 rows form the pattern

113   114

Embossed Leaf Pattern (2)

Multiple of 8 + 1

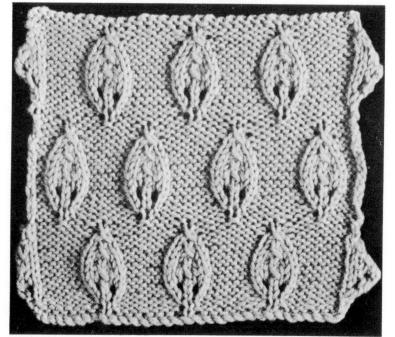

114a

1st row + K.1, P.7, rep. from + K.1.

2nd row + P.1, K.7, rep. from + P.1.

3rd row + K.1, M.1K., P.7, M.1K., rep. from + K.1.

4th row + P.2, K.7, P.1, rep. from + P.1.

5th row + K.1, w.f., K.1, P.7, K.1, w.f., rep. from + K.1.

6th row + P.3, K.7, P.2, rep. from + P.1.

7th row + K.1, w.f., K.2, P.7, K.2, w.f., rep. from + K.1.

8th row + P.4, K.7, P.3, rep. from + P.1.

9th row K.2 tog., K.2, + P.7, K.2, sl.1, K.2 tog., p.s.s.o., K.2, rep. from + P.7, K.2, K.2 tog. t.b.l.

10th row As 6th.

11th row K.2 tog., K.1, + P.7, K.1, sl.1, K.2 tog., p.s.s.o., K.1, rep. from + P.7, K.1, K.2 tog. t.b.l.

12th row As 4th.

13th row K.2 tog., + P.7, sl.1, K.2 tog., p.s.s.o., rep. from + P.7, K.2 tog. t.b.l.

14th row As 2nd.

15th row + P.4, K.1, P.3, rep. from + P.1.

16th row + K.4, P.1, K.3, rep. from + K.1.

17th row + P.4, M.1K., K.1, M.1K., P.3, rep. from + P.1.

18th row + K.4, P.3, K.3, rep. from + K.1.

19th row + P.4, K.1, (w.f., K.1) twice, P.3, rep. from + P.1.

20th row + K.4, P.5, K.3, rep. from + K.1.

21st row + P.4, K.2, w.f., K.1, w.f., K.2, P.3, rep. from + P.1.

22nd row + K.4, P.7, K.3, rep. from + K.1.

23rd row + P.4, K.2, sl.1, K.2 tog., p.s.s.o., K.2, P.3, rep. from + P.1.

24th row   As 20th.

25th row   + P.4, K.1, sl.1, K.2 tog., p.s.s.o., K.1, P.3, rep. from + P.1.

26th row   As 18th.

27th row   + P.4, sl.1, K.2 tog., p.s.s.o., P.3, rep. from + P.1.

28th row   + K.4, P.1, K.3, rep. from + K.1.

These 28 rows form the pattern

Simple Lace Pattern
Multiple of 6 + 1

1st row   (Wrong side) + P.B.2, P.3, P.B.1, rep. from + P.B.1.

2nd row   + K.B.2, w.f., sl.1, K.2 tog., p.s.s.o., w.f., K.B.1, rep. from + K.B.1.

3rd row   As 1st.

4th row   + K.B.2, K.3, K.B.1, rep. from + K.B.1.

These 4 rows form the pattern

115

Umbrella Pattern
Multiple of 18 + 1

1st row   (Wrong side) + P.1, (P.B.1, K.3) 4 times, P.B.1, rep. from + P.1.

2nd row   + K.1, w.f., K.B.1, P.2 tog., P.1, (K.B.1, P.3) twice, K.B.1, P.1, P.2 tog., K.B.1, w.f., rep. from + K.1.

3rd row   + P.2, P.B.1, K.2, (P.B.1, K.3) twice, P.B.1, K.2, P.B.1, P.1, rep. from + P.1.

4th row   + K.2, w.f., K.B.1, P.2, (K.B.1, P.1, P.2 tog.) twice, K.B.1, P.2, K.B.1, w.f., K.1, rep. from + K.1.

5th row   + P.3, (P.B.1, K.2) 4 times, P.B.1, P.2, rep. from + P.1.

6th row   + K.3, w.f., K.B.1, P.2 tog., (K.B.1, P.2) twice, K.B.1, P.2 tog., K.B.1, w.f., K.2, rep. from + K.1.

7th row   + P.4, P.B.1, K.1, (P.B.1, K.2) twice, P.B.1, K.1, P.B.1, P.3, rep. from + P.1.

8th row   + K.4, w.f., K.B.1, P.1, (K.B.1, P.2 tog.) twice, K.B.1, P.1, K.B.1, w.f., K.3, rep. from + K.1.

9th row   + P.5, (P.B.1, K.1) 4 times, P.B.1, P.4, rep. from + P.1.

10th row   + K.5, w.f., K.2 tog. t.b.l., (K.B.1, P.1) twice, K.B.1, K.2 tog., w.f., K.4, rep. from + K.1.

116

11th row + P.6, P.B.2, K.1, P.B.1, K.1, P.B.2, P.5, rep. from + P.1.

12th row + K.6, K.B.2, P.1, K.B.1, P.1, K.B.2, K.5, rep. from + K.1.

These 12 rows form the pattern

Lace Rib Pattern

Multiple of 5 + 3

1st row (Wrong side) + K.3, P.B.2, rep. from + K.3.

2nd row + P.3, K.B.2, w.r.n., rep. from + P.3.

3rd row + K.3, P.B.3, rep. from + K.3.

4th row + P.3, K.B.3, w.r.n., rep. from + P.3.

5th row + K.3, P.B.4, rep. from + K.3.

6th row + P.3, K.B.2, K.2 tog., rep. from + P.3.

7th row As 3rd.

8th row + P.3, K.B.1, K.2 tog., rep. from + P.3.

These 8 rows form the pattern

117

Bavarian Basket Pattern

Multiple of 18 + 7

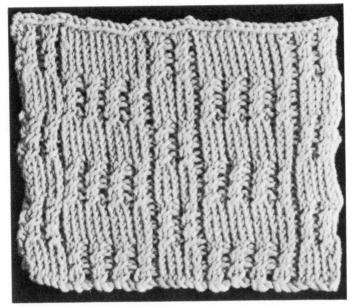

118

1st row + P.1, K.B.5, (P.1, Tw.2) 4 times, rep.
from + P.1, K.B.5, P.1.

2nd row + K.1, P.B.5, (K.1, P.2) 4 times, rep.
from + K.1, P.B.5, K.1.

3rd–6th rows Rep. 1st & 2nd twice.

7th row + (P.1, Tw.2) twice, P.1, K.B.11, rep.
from + (P.1, Tw.2) twice, P.1.

8th row + (K.1, P.2) twice, K.1, P.B.11, rep.
from + (K.1, P.2) twice, K.1.

9th–12th rows Rep. 7th & 8th twice.

These 12 rows form the pattern

Bavarian Block Pattern   (*see page 118*)

Multiple of 14 + 4

1st & 2nd rows Knit.

3rd row + P.1, Tw.2, P.1, K.B.10, rep. from +
P.1, Tw.2, P.1.

4th row + K.1, P.2, K.1, P.B.10, rep. from +
K.1, P.2, K.1.

5th–8th rows Rep. 3rd & 4th twice.

9th & 10th rows Knit.

11th row + K.B.7, P.1, Tw.2, P.1, K.B.3, rep.
from + K.B.4.

12th row + P.B.7, K.1, P.2, K.1, P.B.3, rep. from
+ P.B.4.

13th–16th rows Rep. 11th & 12th twice.

These 16 rows form the pattern

119

Bavarian Check Pattern

Multiple of 18 + 10

120

1st row + (P.1, Tw.2) 3 times, P.1, K.B.8, rep. from + (P.1, Tw.2) 3 times, P.1.

2nd row + (K.1, P.2) 3 times, K.1, P.B.8, rep. from + (K.1, P.2) 3 times, K.1.

3rd–10th rows Rep. 1st & 2nd four times.

11th row P.1, + K.B.8, (P.1, Tw.2) 3 times, P.1, rep. from + K.B.8, P.1.

12th row K.1, + P.B.8, (K.1, P.2) 3 times, K.1, rep. from + P.B.8, K.1.

13th–20th rows Rep. 11th & 12th four times.

These 20 rows form the pattern

118

Bavarian Diamond Pattern

Multiple of 18 + 1

121

1st row P.I, + (Tw.2, P.I) 3 times, K.B.2, (P.I, Tw.2) twice, P.I, rep. from +.

2nd row K.I. + (P.2, K.I) twice, P.B.2, (K.I, P.2) 3 times, K.I, rep. from +.

3rd & 4th rows As 1st & 2nd.

5th row P.I, + (Tw.2, P.I) twice, K.B.8, P.I, Tw.2, P.I, rep. from +.

6th row K.I, + P.2, K.I, P.B.8, K.I, (P.2, K.I) twice, rep. from +.

7th & 8th rows As 5th & 6th.

9th row P.I, + Tw.2, P.I, K.B.14, P.I, rep. from +.

10th row K.I, + P.B.14, K.I, P.2, K.I, rep. from +.

11th & 12th rows As 9th & 10th.

13th–16th rows Rep. 5th & 6th twice.

These 16 rows form the pattern

119

AUSTRIAN

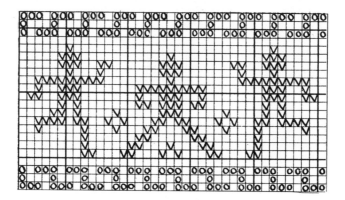

122

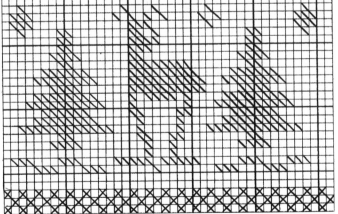

123

124

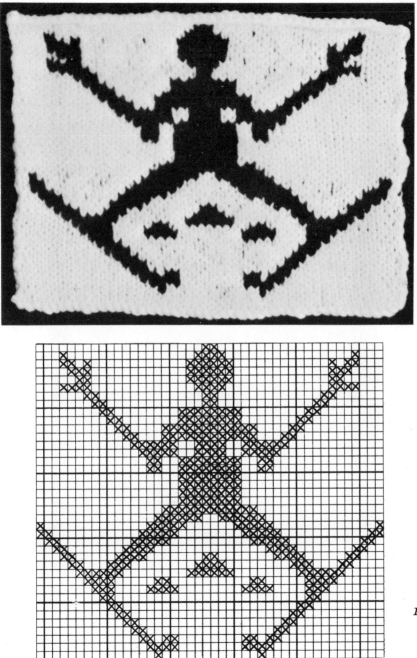

125

AUSTRIAN KNITTING PATTERNS

Tyrolean Diamond Pattern

Cast on 21 sts.

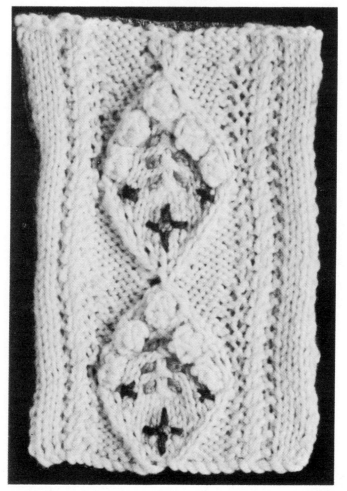

126

1st row   P.1, Tw.2, P.5, K.2 tog., M.1K., K.1, M.1K., K.2 tog. t.b.l., P.5, Tw.2, P.1.

2nd row   P.4, K.4, P.5, K.4, P.4.

3rd row   P.1, Tw.2, P.1, P.3, K.2 tog., M.1K, K.3, M.1K, K.2 tog. t.b.l., P.4, Tw.2, P.1.

4th row   P.4, K.3, P.7, K.3, P.4.

5th row   P.1, Tw.2, P.3, K.2 tog., M.1K, K.5, M.1K, K.2 tog. t.b.l., P.3, Tw.2, P.1.

6th row   P.4, K.2, P.9, K.2, P.4.

7th row P.1, Tw.2, P.2, K.2 tog., M.1K, K.7, M.1K, K.2 tog. t.b.l., P.2, Tw.2, P.1.

8th row P.4, K.1, P.11, K.1, P.4.

9th row P.1, Tw.2, P.1, K.2 tog., M.1K, K.9, M.1K, K.2 tog. t.b.l., P.1, Tw.2, P.1.

10th row Purl.

11th row P.1, Tw.2, inc. by purling into front and back of next st., K.1, M.B., K.3, sl.1, K.2 tog., p.s.s.o., K.3, M.B., K.1, inc. in next st., Tw.2, P.1.

12th row As 8th.

13th row P.1, Tw.2, P.1, inc. in next st., K.4, sl.1, K.2 tog., p.s.s.o., K.4, inc. in next st., P.1, Tw.2, P.1.

14th row As 6th.

15th row P.1, Tw.2, P.1, inc. in next st., P.1, K.1, M.B., K.1, sl.1, K.2 tog., p.s.s.o., K.1, M.B., K.1, P.1, inc. in next st., P.1, Tw.2, P.1.

16th row As 4th.

17th row P.1, Tw.2, P.1, inc. in next st., P.2, K.2, sl.1, K.2 tog., p.s.s.o., K.2, P.2, inc. in next st., P.1, Tw.2, P.1.

18th row As 2nd.

19th row P.1, Tw.2, P.1, inc. in next st., P.3, K.2 tog. t.b.l., M.B., K.2 tog., P.3, inc. in next st., P.1, Tw.2, P.1.

20th row P.4, K.5, P.3, K.5, P.4.

21st row P.1, Tw.2, P.1, inc. in next st., P.4, sl.1, K.2 tog., p.s.s.o., P.4, inc. in next st., P.1, Tw.2, P.1.

22nd row P.4, K.6, P.1, K.6, P.4.

23rd row P.1, Tw.2, P.5, P.2 tog., M.1K., K.1, M.1K., P.2 tog., P.5, Tw.2, P.1.

24th row P.4, K.5, P.3, K.5, P.4.

These 24 rows form the pattern

Tyrolean Fern Pattern

Cast on 29 sts.

1st row K.1, Tw.2F., Tw.2B., K.1, P.5, Tw.2B., K.1, M.B., K.1, Tw.2F., P.5, K.1, Tw.2F., Tw.2B., K.1.

2nd row K.1, P.4, K.6, P.7, K.6, P.4, K.1.

3rd row K.1, Tw.2B., Tw.2F., K.1, P.4, Tw.2B., K.5, Tw.2F., P.4, K.1, Tw.2B., Tw.2F., K.1.

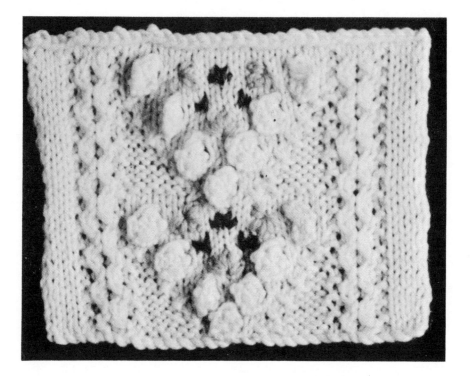

127

4th row   K.1, P.4, K.5, P.9, K.5, P.4, K.1.

5th row   K.1, Tw.2F., Tw.2B., K.1, P.3, Tw.2B., K.1, M.B., K.3, M.B., K.1, Tw.2F., P.3, K.1, Tw.2F., Tw.2B., K.1.

6th row   K.1, P.4, K.4, P.11, K.4, P.4, K.1.

7th row   K.1, Tw.2B., Tw.2F., K.1, P.2, Tw.2B., K.9, Tw.2F., P.2, K.1, Tw.2B., Tw.2F., K.1.

8th row   K.1, P.4, K.3, P.13, K.3, P.4, K.1.

9th row   K.1, Tw.2F., Tw.2B., K.1, P.1, Tw.2B., K.1, M.B., K.7, M.B., K.1, Tw.2F., P.1, K.1, Tw.2F., Tw.2B., K.1.

10th row   K.1, P.4, K.2, P.15, K.2, P.4, K.1.

11th row   K.1, Tw.2B., Tw.2F., K.1, Tw.2B., K.13, Tw.2F., K.1, Tw.2B., Tw.2F., K.1.

12th row   K.1, P.4, K.1, P.17, K.1, P.4, K.1.

13th row   K.1, Tw.2F., Tw.2B., K.3, M.B., K.11, M.B., K.3, Tw.2F., Tw.2B., K.1.

14th row   As 12th.

15th row   K.1, Tw.2B., Tw.2F., K.19, Tw.2B., Tw.2F., K.1.

16th row   As 12th.

These 16 rows form the pattern

Tyrolean Leaf Pattern

Cast on 25 sts.

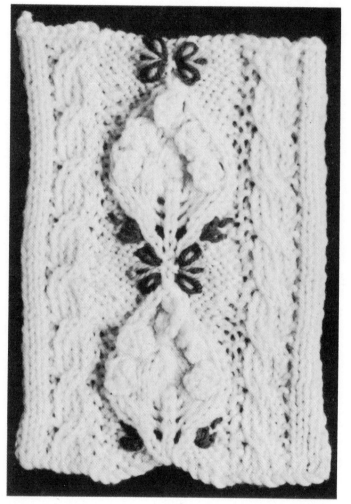

128

1st row K.1, K.B.4, K.1, P.2 tog., P.4, M.1K., K.1, M.1K., P.4, P.2 tog., K.1, K.B.4, K.1.

2nd row K.1, P.B.4, K.6, P.3, K.6, P.B.4, K.1.

3rd row K.1, K.B.4, K.1, P.2 tog., P.3, (K.1, w.f.) twice, K.1, P.3, P.2 tog., K.1, K.B.4, K.1.

4th row K.1, P.B.4, K.5, P.5, K.5, P.B.4, K.1.

5th row K.1, CB.2F., K.1, P.2 tog., P.2, K.2, w.f., K.1, w.f., K.2, P.2, P.2 tog., K.1, CB.2B., K.1.

6th row K.1, P.B.4, K.4, P.7, K.4, P.B.4, K.1.

7th row   K.1, K.B.4, K.1, P.2 tog., P.1, K.3, w.f., K.1, w.f., K.3, P.1, P.2 tog., K.1, K.B.4, K.1.

8th row   K.1, P.B.4, K.3, P.9, K.3, P.B.4, K.1.

9th row   K.1, K.B.4, K.1, P.2 tog., K.4, w.f., K.1, w.f., K.4, P.2 tog., K.1, K.B.4, K.1.

10th row   K.1, P.B.4, K.2, P.11, K.2, P.B.4, K.1.

11th row   K.1, CB.2F., K.1, P.1, K.1, M.B., K.7, M.B., K.1, P.1, K.1, C.B.2B., K.1.

12th row   As 10th.

13th row   K.1, K.B.4, K.1, inc. by purling into front and back of next st., K.4, sl.1, K.2 tog., p.s.s.o., K.4, inc. in next st., K.1, K.B.4, K.1.

14th row   As 8th.

15th row   K.1, K.B.4, K.1, inc. in next st., P.1, K.1, M.B., K.1, sl.1, K.2 tog., p.s.s.o., K.1, M.B., K.1, P.1, inc. in next st., K.1, K.B.4, K.1.

16th row   As 6th.

17th row   K.1, CB.2F., K.1, inc. in next st., P.2, K.2, sl.1, K.2 tog., p.s.s.o., K.2, P.2, inc. in next st., K.1, CB.2B., K.1.

18th row   As 4th.

19th row   K.1, K.B.4, K.1, inc. in next st., P.3, K.2 tog. t.b.l., M.B., K.2 tog., P.3, inc. in next st., K.1, K.B.4, K.1.

20th row   As 2nd.

21st row   K.1, K.B.4, K.1, inc. in next st., P.4, sl.1, K.2 tog., p.s.s.o., P.4, inc. in next st., K.1, K.B.4, K.1.

22nd row   K.1, P.B.4, K.7, P.1, K.7, P.B.4, K.1.

23rd row   K.1, CB.2F., K.1, P.13, K.1, CB.2B., K.1.

24th row   K.1, P.B.4, K.15, P.B.4, K.1.

These 24 rows form the pattern

Tyrolean Cable and Bobble Pattern

Cast on 29 sts.

1st row   K.1, Tw.3, K.1, P.2, CB.3B., K.3, CB.3F., P.2, K.1, Tw.3, K.1.

2nd & every alt. row   K.1, P.3, K.3, P.B.6, P.3, P.B.6, K.3, P.3, K.1.

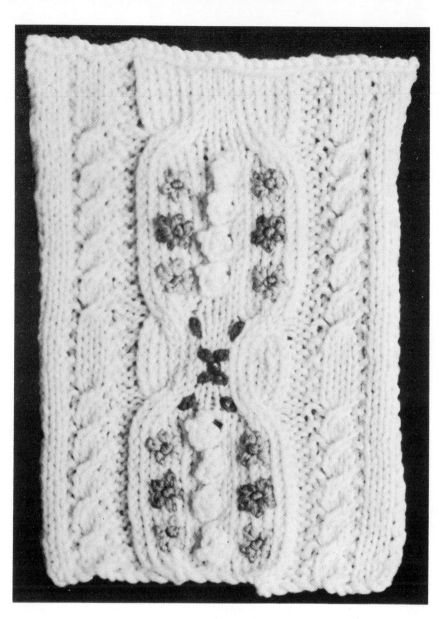

129

3rd row K.5, P.2, K.B.6, K.3, K.B.6, P.2, K.5.	*9th–20th rows* Rep. 5–8 three times.
5th row K.1, Tw.3, K.1, P.2, K.B.6, K.1, M.B., K.1, K.B.6, P.2, K.1, Tw.3, K.1.	*21st row* K.1, Tw.3, K.1, P.2, CB.3F., K.3, CB.3B., P.2, K.1, Tw.3, K.1.
7th row K.5, P.2, K.B.6, K.3, K.B.6, P.2, K.5.	*23rd row* As 3rd.
8th row As 2nd.	*25th–30th rows* Rep. 3rd & 4th three times.

These 30 rows form the pattern

Lace Mats
ABBREVIATIONS

O   K.

| w.f.

U   sl.1, K.2 tog., p.s.s.o.

ᑎ   sl.1, K.1, p.s.s.o.

ᐱ   K.2 tog.

{   K.B.1.

▢   No stitch.

→   Slip first st. from left-hand needle on to right-hand needle, then commence patt. Do this on all needles.

⇥   Slip first 3 sts. from left-hand needle on to right-hand needle, then commence patt. Do this on all needles.

✕   Crochet edge.

Round Mat
Worked with 4 needles

Cast on 3 sts. on first and second needle and 2 sts. on third needle.

1st round   Knit.

2nd & every alt. round   Knit.

3rd round   + w.f., K.1, rep. from +.

5th round   + w.f., K.1, rep. from +.

7th round   + w.f., K.3, w.f., K.1, rep. from +.

9th round   + w.f., K.1, sl.1, K.2 tog., p.s.s.o., K.1, w.f., K.1, rep. from +.

10th round   Knit.

Continue to work from chart.

Square Mat
Worked with 5 needles

Cast on 2 sts. on each of 4 needles.

1st round   Knit.

2nd & every alt. round   Knit.

3rd round   + K.B.1, w.f., K.1, w.f., rep. from +.

5th round   + K.B.1, w.f., K.3, w.f., rep. from +.

7th round   + K.B.1, w.f., K.5, w.f., rep. from +.

9th round + K.B.1, w.f., K.1, K.2 tog., w.f., K.1, w.f., sl.1, K.1, p.s.s.o., K.1, w.f., rep. from +.

11th round + K.B.1, w.f., K.1, K.2 tog., w.f., K.3, w.f., sl.1, K.1, p.s.s.o., K.1, w.f., rep. from +.

13th round + K.B.1, w.f., K.3, w.f., K.5, w.f., K.3, w.f., rep. from +.

14th round Knit.

Continue to work from chart.

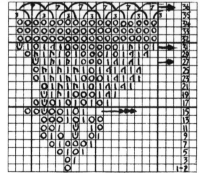

130

131

131

V

Dutch Knitting

ALTHOUGH HOLLAND borders on both Germany and France there is little sign of the knitting in either of these countries having influenced Dutch traditional patterns. These are, in essence, simple and austere, reflecting the living background of the Dutch household.

It is not known when knitting started to be practised in Holland. We do know the Dutch people were famous for their quilting, the use of fine lines of stitching to create embossed shapes, and patterns on fabric. The quilting patterns certainly influenced the development of knitting patterns and we find that most of the traditional stitches try to copy the same principles in design as Dutch quilting.

In many of the historical examples of quilted bedspreads we find that when the quilting was completed the centre of the squares, diamonds and other shapes that form the basic design were then embroidered with birds and flowers, the embroidery being padded to give an embossed effect to the finished design.

In the seventeenth and eighteenth centuries the Dutch specialised in embossed knitting, the patterns being in twisted stocking-stitch on a reverse stocking-stitch ground. A very fine example of this type of knitting, in the collection at the Victoria and Albert Museum, consists of a knitted cotton petticoat that is literally covered with embossed birds, beasts, flowers and trees, and at first sight looks much more like a piece of woven and embroidered fabric than a specimen of hand knitting.

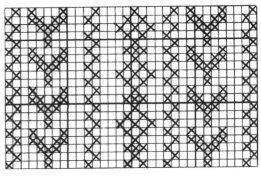

132

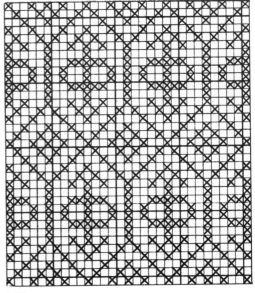

133

134

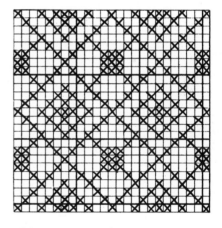

135

Pyramid Pattern

Multiple of 15 + 7

136

1st row + P.1, K.B.5, P.1, K.8, rep. from + P.1, K.B.5, P.1.

2nd row + K.1, P.B.5, K.1, P.8, rep. from + K.1, P.B.5, K.1.

3rd row + P.1, K.B.5, P.9, rep. from + P.1, K.B.5, P.1.

4th row + K.1, P.B.5, K.9, rep. from + K.1, P.B.5, K.1.

5th row + P.2, K.B.3, P.3, K.6, P.1, rep. from + P.2, K.B.3, P.2.

6th row + K.2, P.B.3, K.3, P.6, K.1, rep. from + K.2, P.B.3, K.2.

7th row + P.2, K.B.3, P.10, rep. from + P.2, K.B.3, P.2.

8th row + K.2, P.B.3, K.10, rep. from + K.2, P.B.3, K.2.

9th row + P.3, K.B.1, P.5, K.4, P.2, rep. from + P.3, K.B.1, P.3.

10th row + K.3, P.B.1, K.5, P.4, K.2, rep. from + K.3, P.B.1, K.3.

11th row + P.3, K.B.1, P.11, rep. from + P.3, K.B.1, P.3.

12th row + K.3, P.B.1, K.11, rep. from + K.3, P.B.1, K.3.

These 12 rows form the pattern

Squared Chequer Pattern

Multiple of 10 + 2

1st row Knit.

2nd row Purl.

3rd row + K.2, P.8, rep. from + K.2.

4th row + P.2, K.8, rep. from + P.2.

5th row + K.2, P.2, K.B.4, P.2, rep. from + K.2.

6th row + P.2, K.2, P.B.4, K.2, rep. from + P.2.

7th–10th rows Rep. 5th & 6th twice.

11th & 12th rows As 3rd & 4th.

These 12 rows form the pattern

137

Diamond Knot Pattern
Multiple of 14 + 2

138

1st row Knit.

2nd row Purl.

3rd row + K.2, P.12, rep. from + K.2.

4th row + P.2, K.12, rep. from + P.2.

5th row + K.2, P.5, K.B.2, P.5, rep. from + K.2.

6th row + P.2, K.5, P.B.2, K.5, rep. from + P.2.

7th row + K.2, P.4, K.B.4, P.4, rep. from + K.2.

8th row + P.2, K.4, P.B.4, K.4, rep. from + P.2.

9th row + K.2, P.3, K.B.6, P.3, rep. from + K.2.

10th row + P.2, K.3, P.B.6, K.3, rep. from + P.2.

11th row + K.2, P.2, K.B.1, CB.3B., K.B.1, P.2, rep. from + K.2.

12th row + P.2, K.2, P.B.8, K.2, rep. from + P.2.

13th & 14th rows As 9th & 10th.

15th & 16th rows As 7th & 8th.

17th & 18th rows As 5th & 6th.

19th & 20th rows As 3rd & 4th.

These 20 rows form the pattern

Quartered Diamond Pattern
Multiple of 18 + 1

139

1st row Purl.

2nd row Knit.

3rd row + P.9, K.B.1, P.8, rep. from + P.1.

4th row + K.8, P.B.3, K.7, rep. from + K.1.

5th row + P.7, K.B.5, P.6, rep. from + P.1.

6th row As 4th.

7th row + P.5, (K.B.1, P.3) twice, K.B.1, P.4, rep. from + P.1.

8th row + K.4, P.B.3, K.5, P.B.3, K.3, rep. from + K.1.

9th row + P.3, K.B.5, P.3, K.B.5, P.2, rep. from + P.1.

10th–17th rows Rep. rows 8–1.

18th row Knit.

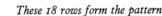

These 18 rows form the pattern

Ladder and Diamond Pattern
Multiple of 14 + 7

1st row + Tw.2, P.3, Tw.2, P.3, K.B.1, P.3, rep. from + Tw.2, P.3, Tw.2.

2nd row + P.2, K.3, P.2, K.3, P.B.1, K.3, rep. from + P.2, K.3, P.2.

3rd row + Tw.2, K.3, Tw.2, P.2, K.B.3, P.2, rep. from + Tw.2, K.3, Tw.2.

4th row + P.7, K.2, P.B.3, K.2, rep. from + P.7.

5th row + Tw.2, P.3, Tw.2, P.1, K.B.5, P.1, rep. from + Tw.2, P.3, Tw.2.

140

6th row　+ P.2, K.3, P.2, K.1, P.B.5, K.1, rep. from + P.2, K.3, P.2.

7th row　+ Tw.2, K.3, Tw.2, P.1, K.B.5, P.1, rep. from + Tw.2, K.3, Tw.2.

8th row　+ P.7, K.2, P.B.3, K.2, rep. from + P.7.

9th row　+ Tw.2, P.3, Tw.2, P.2, K.B.3, P.2, rep. from + Tw.2, P.3, Tw.2.

10th row　+ P.2, K.3, P.2, K.3, P.B.1, K.3, rep. from + P.2, K.3, P.2.

11th row　+ Tw.2, K.3, Tw.2, P.3, K.B.1, P.3, rep. from + Tw.2. K.3, Tw.2.

12th row　+ P.7, K.7, rep. from + P.7.

These 12 rows form the pattern

Hexagonal Quilting Pattern
Multiple of 14 + 1

141

1st row　+ K.4, P.7, K.3, rep. from + K.1.

2nd row　+ P.3, K.9, P.2, rep. from + P.1.

3rd row　+ K.2, P.4, K.B.3, P.4, K.1, rep. from + K.1.

4th row　+ P.1, K.4, P.B.5, K.4, rep. from + P.1.

5th row　+ P.4, K.B.2, P.3, K.B.2, P.3, rep. from + P.1.

6th row　+ K.3, P.B.2, K.5, P.B.2, K.2, rep. from + K.1.

7th row + P.2, K.B.2, P.7, K.B.2, P.1, rep. from + P.1.

8th row + K.2, P.B.2, K.7, P.B.2, K.1, rep. from + K.1.

9th row As 7th.

10th & 11th rows As 6th & 5th.

12th & 13th rows As 4th & 3rd.

14th row As 2nd.

These 14 rows form the pattern

Quilted Leaf Pattern
Multiple of 18 + 7

142

1st row + P.1, Tw.2, rep. from + P.1.

2nd row + K.1, P.2, rep. from + K.1.

3rd & 4th rows As 1st & 2nd.

5th row + (P.1. Tw.2) twice, P.4, P.2 tog., w.o.n., K.B.1, w.r.n., P.2 tog., P.3, rep. from + (P.1, Tw. 2) twice, P.1.

6th row + (K.1, P.2) twice, K.5, P.B.3, K.4, rep. from + (K.1, P.2) twice, K.1.

7th row + (P.1, Tw.2) twice, P.3, P.2 tog., w.o.n., K.B.3, w.r.n., P.2 tog., P.2, rep. from + (P.1, Tw.2) twice, P.1.

8th row + (K.1, P.2) twice, K.4, P.B.5, K.3, rep. from + (K.1, P.2) twice, K.1.

9th row + (P.1, Tw.2) twice, P.2, P.2 tog., w.o.n., K.B.5, w.r.n., P.2 tog., P.1, rep. from + (P.1, Tw.2) twice, P.1.

10th row + (K.1, P.2) twice, K.3, P.B.7, K.2, rep. from + (K.1, P.2) twice, K.1.

11th row + (P.1, Tw.2) twice, P.3, w.o.n., K.B.2, sl.1, K.2 tog., p.s.s.o., K.B.2, w.r.n., P.2, rep. from + (P.1, Tw.2) twice, P.1.

12th row As 8th.

13th row + (P.1, Tw.2) twice, P.4, w.o.n., K.B.1, sl.1, K.2 tog., p.s.s.o., K.B.1, w.r.n., P.3, rep. from + (P.1, Tw.2) twice, P.1.

14th row As 6th.

15th row + (P.1, Tw.2) twice, P.5, w.o.n., sl.1, K.2 tog., p.s.s.o., w.r.n., P.4, rep. from + (P.1, Tw.2) twice, P.1.

16th row + (K.1, P.2) twice, K.6, P.B.1, K.5, rep. from + (K.1, P.2) twice, K.1.

These 16 rows form the pattern

Ladder and Feather Pattern
Multiple of 34 + 15

143

1st row + P.2, K.B.2, P.2, Tw.3, P.2, K.B.2, P.2, K.3 tog., K.5, (w.f., K.1) 3 times, w.f., K.5, K.3 tog. t.b.l., rep. from + P.2, K.B.2, P.2, Tw.3, P.2, K.B.2, P.2.

2nd row + K.2, P.B.2, K.2, P.3, K.2, P.B.2, K.2, P.19, rep. from + K.2, P.B.2, K.2, P.3, K.2, P.B.2, K.2.

3rd row + P.6, K.3, P.6, K.3 tog., K.4, w.f., K.1, w.f., K.3, w.f., K.1, w.f., K.4, K.3 tog. t.b.l., rep. from + P.6, K.3, P.6.

4th row + K.6, P.3, K.6, P.19, rep. from + K.6, P.3, K.6.

5th row + P.2, K.B.2, P.2, Tw.3, P.2, K.B.2, P.2, K.3 tog., K.3, w.f., K.1, w.f., K.5, w.f., K.1, w.f., K.3, K.3 tog. t.b.l., P.2, K.B.2, P.2, Tw.3, P.2, K.B.2, P.2.

6th row As 2nd.

7th row + P.6, K.3, P.6, K.3 tog., K.2, w.f., K.1, w.f., K.7, w.f., K.1, w.f., K.2, K.3 tog. t.b.l., P.6, K.3, P.6.

8th row As 4th.

9th row + P.2, K.B.2, P.2, Tw.3, P.2, K.B.2, P.2, K.3 tog., K.1, w.f., K.1, w.f., K.9, (w.f.,

K.1) twice, K.3 tog. t.b.l., rep. from + P.2, K.B.2, P.2, Tw.3, P.2, K.B.2, P.2.

10th row As 2nd.

11th row + P.6, K.3, P.6, K.19, rep. from + P.6, K.3, P.6.

12th row + K.6, P.3, K.6, P.19, rep. from + K.6, P.3, K.6.

These 12 rows form the pattern

Lace and Diamond Pattern
Multiple of 18 + 9

144

1st row + (P.1, K.3) twice, P.1, K.2, K.2 tog., w.f., K.1, w.f., K.2 tog. t.b.l., K.2, rep. from + (P.1, K.3) twice, P.1.

2nd row + (K.1, P.3) twice, K.1, P.9, rep. from + (K.1, P.3) twice, K.1.

3rd row + P.1, K.2, P.1, K.1, P.1, K.2, P.1, K.1, K.2 tog., w.f., K.3, w.f., K.2 tog. t.b.l., K.1, rep. from + P.1, K.2, P.1, K.1, P.1, K.2, P.1.

4th row + K.1, P.2, K.1, P.1, K.1, P.2, K.1, P.9, rep. from + K.1, P.2, K.1, P.1, K.1, P.2, K.1.

5th row + (P.1, K.1) 4 times, P.1, K.2 tog., w.f.,

K.5, w.f., K.2 tog. t.b.l., rep. from + (P.1, K.1) 4 times, P.1.

6th row + (K.1, P.1) 4 times, K.1, P.9, rep. from + (K.1, P.1) 4 times, K.1.

7th row + P.1, K.2, P.1, K.1, P.1, K.2, P.1, K.2 tog., w.f., K.5, w.f., K.2 tog. t.b.l., rep. from + P.1, K.2, P.1, K.1, P.1, K.2, P.1.

8th row As 4th.

9th row + (P.1, K.3) twice, P.1, K.3, w.f., sl.1, K.2 tog., p.s.s.o., w.f., K.3, rep. from + (P.1, K.3) twice, P.1.

10th row + (K.1, P.3) twice, K.1, P.9, rep. from + (K.1, P.3) twice, K.1.

These 10 rows form the pattern

Vandyke and Lace Pattern
Multiple of 20 + 11

1st row + P.1, K.B.1, P.7, K.B.1, P.1, w.o.n., K.2 tog. t.b.l., K.5, K.2 tog., w.r.n., rep. from + P.1, K.B.1, P.7, K.B.1, P.1.

2nd row + K.1, P.B.2, K.5, P.B.2, K.1, P.9, rep. from + K.1, P.B.2, K.5, P.B.2, K.1.

3rd row + P.1, K.B.3, P.3, K.B.3, P.1, K.1, w.f., K.2 tog. t.b.l., K.3, K.2 tog., w.f., K.1, rep. from + P.1, K.B.3, P.3, K.B.3, P.1.

4th row + (K.1, P.B.4) twice, K.1, P.9, rep. from + (K.1, P.B.4) twice, K.1.

145

5th row + P.2, K.B.7, P.2, K.2, w.f., K.2 tog. t.b.l., K.1, K.2 tog., w.f., K.2, rep. from + P.2, K.B.7, P.2.

5th row + P.2, K.B.7, P.2, K.2, w.f., K.2 tog. t.b.l., K.1, K.2 tog., w.f., K.2, rep. from + P.2, K.B.7, P.2.

6th row + K.3, P.B.5, K.3, P.9, rep. from + K.3, P.B.5, K.3.

7th row + P.4, K.B.3, P.4, K.3, w.f., sl.1, K.2 tog., p.s.s.o., w.f., K.3, rep. from + P.4, K.B.3, P.4.

8th row + K.5, P.B.1, K.5, P.9, rep. from + K.5, P.B.1, K.5.

These 8 rows form the pattern

Chequer and Lace Pattern   (*see page 145*)

Multiple of 17 + 10

1st row + P.1, K.B.3, P.2, K.B.3, P.1, K.1, K.2 tog., w.f., K.1, w.f., K.2 tog. t.b.l., K.1, rep. from + P.1, K.B.3, P.2, K.B.3, P.1.

2nd row + K.1, P.B.3, K.2, P.B.3, K.1, P.7, rep. from + K.1, P.B.3, K.2, P.B.3, K.1.

3rd row + P.1, K.B.1, P.2, K.B.2, P.2, K.B.1, P.1, K.2 tog., w.f., K.3, w.f., K.2 tog. t.b.l., rep. from + P.1, K.B.1, P.2, K.B.2, P.2, K.B.1, P.1.

4th row + K.1, P.B.1, K.2, P.B.2, K.2, P.B.1, K.1, P.7, rep. from + K.1, P.B.1, K.2, P.B.2, K.2, P.B.1, K.1.

These 4 rows form the pattern

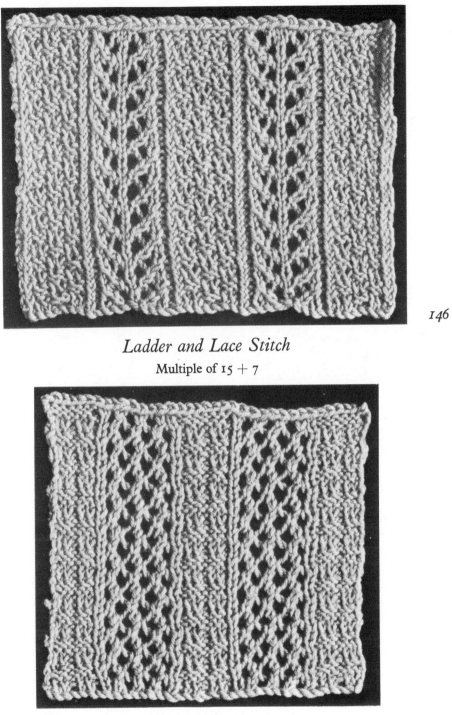

146

Ladder and Lace Stitch

Multiple of 15 + 7

146a

1st row + (P.1, K.B.2) twice, P.1, K.1, (w.f., K.2 tog.) 3 times, K.1, rep. from + (P.1, K.B.2) twice, P.1.

2nd row + (K.1, P.B.2) twice, K.1, P.8, rep. from + (K.1, P.B.2) twice, K.1.

3rd row + P.7, K.1, (K.2 tog., w.f.) 3 times, K.1, rep. from + P.7.

4th row + K.7, P.8, rep. from + K.7.

These 4 rows form the pattern

Marriage Lines Lace Pattern
Multiple of 14 + 7

147

1st row + P.7, K.1, w.f., K.2 tog., K.4, rep. from + P.7.

2nd & every alt. row + (K.1, P.B.1) 3 times, K.1, P.7, rep. from + (K.1, P.B.1) 3 times, K.1.

3rd row + P.7, K.2, w.f., K.2 tog., K.3, rep. from + P.7.

5th row + P.7, K.3, w.f., K.2 tog., K.2, rep. from + P.7.

7th row + P.7, K.4, w.f., K.2 tog., K.1, rep. from + P.7.

9th row + P.7, K.3, K.2 tog. t.b.l., w.f., K.2, rep. from + P.7.

11th row   + P.7, K.2, K.2 tog. t.b.l., w.f., K.3, rep. from + P.7.

13th row   + P.7, K.1, K.2 tog. t.b.l., w.f., K.4, rep. from + P.7.

15th row   + P.7, K.2 tog. t.b.l., w.f., K.5, rep. from + P.7.

16th row   + (K.1, P.B.1) 3 times, K.1, P.7, rep. from + (K.1, P.B.1) 3 times, K.1.

These 16 rows form the pattern

Ladder Stitch Pattern

Multiple of 29 + 10

148

1st row   + P.4, K.B.2, P.4, K.1, w.f., K.2 tog., K.13, K.2 tog. t.b.l., w.f., K.1, rep. from + P.4, K.B.2, P. 4.

2nd row   + K.4, P.B.2, K.4, P.2, w.r.n., P.2 tog. t.b.l., P.11, P.2 tog., w.r.n., P.2, rep. from + K.4, P.B.2, K.4.

3rd row   + P.2, K.B.6, P.2, K.3, w.f., K.2 tog., K.9, K.2 tog. t.b.l., w.f., K.3, rep. from + P.2, K.B.6, P.2.

4th row   + K.2, P.B.6, K.2, P.4, w.r.n., P.2 tog. t.b.l., P.7, P.2 tog., w.r.n., P.4, rep. from + K.2, P.B.6, K.2.

5th row   + P.4, K.B.2, P.4, K.5, w.f., K.2 tog., K.5, K.2 tog. t.b.l., w.f., K.5, rep. from + P.4, K.B.2, P.4.

6th row   + K.4, P.B.2, K.4, P.6, w.r.n., P.2 tog. t.b.l., P.3, P.2 tog., w.r.n., P.6, rep. from + K.4, P.B.2, K.4.

7th row P.2, K.B.6, P.2, K.7, w.f., K.2 tog., K.1, K.2 tog. t.b.l., w.f., K.7, rep. from + P.2, K.B.6, P.2.

8th row + K.2, P.B.6, K.2, P.19, rep. from + K.2, P.B.6, K.2.

These 8 rows form the pattern

Arrow and Lace Pattern
Multiple of 16 + 9

149

1st row + P.4, K.B.1, P.4, K.1, K.2 tog., w.f., K.1, w.f., K.2 tog. t.b.l., K.1, rep. from + P.4, K.B.1, P.4.

2nd row + K.3, P.B.3, K.3, P.7, rep. from + K.3, P.B.3, K.3.

3rd row + P.2, K.B.5, P.2, K.1, K.2 tog., w.f., K.1, w.f., K.2 tog. t.b.l., K.1, rep. from + P.2, K.B.5, P.2.

4th row + K.1, P.B.7, K.1, P.7, rep. from + K.1, P.B.7, K.1.

5th row + P.1, K.B.3, P.1, K.B.3, P.1, K.2, w.f., sl.1, K.2 tog., p.s.s.o., w.f., K.2, rep. from + P.1, K.B.3, P.1, K.B.3, P.1.

148

6th row + K.1, P.B.2, K.3, P.B.2, K.1, P.7, rep. from + K.1, P.B.2, K.3, P.B.2, K.1.

7th row + P.1, K.B.1, P.5, K.B.1, P.1, K.2, w.f., sl.1, K.2 tog., p.s.s.o., w.f., K.2, rep. from + P.1, K.B.1, P.5, K.B.1, P.1.

8th row + K.9, P.7, rep. from + K.9.

These 8 rows form the pattern

Pique Lace Pattern
Multiple of 16 + 7

150

1st row K.B.2, P.1, K.B.1, P.1, K.B.2, K.3, w.f., sl.1, K.2 tog., p.s.s.o., w.f., K.3, rep. from + K.B.2, P.1, K.B.1, P.1, K.B.2.

2nd row + P.B.2, K.1, P.B.1, K.1, P.B.2, P.9, rep. from + P.B.2, K.1, P.B.1, K.1, P.B.2.

3rd row + (K.B.1, P.1) 3 times, K.B.1, K.2, K.2 tog. t.b.l., w.f., K.1, w.f., K.2 tog., K.2, rep. from + (K.B.1, P.1) 3 times, K.B.1.

4th row + (P.B.1, K.1) 3 times, P.B.1, P.9, rep. from + (P.B.1, K.1) 3 times, P.B.1.

5th row + K.B.2, P.1, K.B.1, P.1, K.B.2, K.1, K.2 tog. t.b.l., w.f., sl.1, K.2 tog., p.s.s.o., w.f., K.2 tog., K.1, rep. from + K.B.2, P.1, K.B.1, P.1, K.B.2.

6th row + P.B.2, K.1, P.B.1, K.1, P.B.2, P.2, P. into front and back of w.f. of previous row, P.1, P. into front and back of w.f., P.2, rep. from + P.B.2, K.1, P.B.1, K.1, P.B.2.

7th row + (K.B.1, P.1) 3 times, K.B.1, (K.2 tog. t.b.l., w.f.) twice, K.1, (w.f., K.2 tog.) twice, rep. from + (K.B.1, P.1) 3 times, K.B.1.

8th row + (P.B.1, K.1) 3 times, P.B.1, P.9, rep. from + (P.B.1, K.1) 3 times, P.B.1.

These 8 rows form the pattern

VI

Scandinavian Knitting

KNITTING was undoubtedly practised in Norway as early as the ninth century, as the early immigrants, who travelled from Norway to the Faroes and the Shetlands, took knitting with them as one of their established crafts. In Norway for centuries they have specialised in coloured knitting, using navy, dull red and dark green on a white ground, and these colours are still used in the sweaters in the shops in Oslo at the present time.

The Swedish tradition was undoubtedly developed from the Norwegian knitters' craft, but here the coloured designs become more varied and more sophisticated than the simple patterns one finds in Norwegian designs. There appears to be no native tradition for self-coloured knitting patterns, but one does find variations of patterns from Germany and Holland worked in self colour in various parts of Scandinavia.

In Denmark knitting was unknown until the fifteenth century, when a group of stocking knitters from Holland were invited to settle outside Copenhagen to produce hosiery for the members of the Danish Court. It was these knitters who taught the Danes the craft and even today we find a very strong Dutch influence in Danish knitting.

151

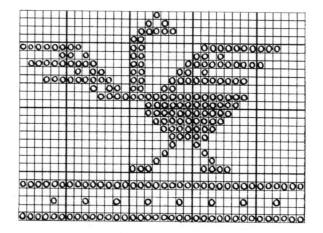

152

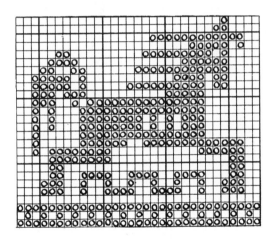

153

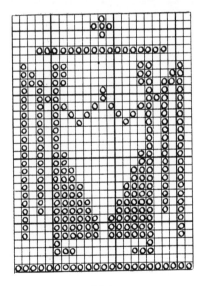

154

155

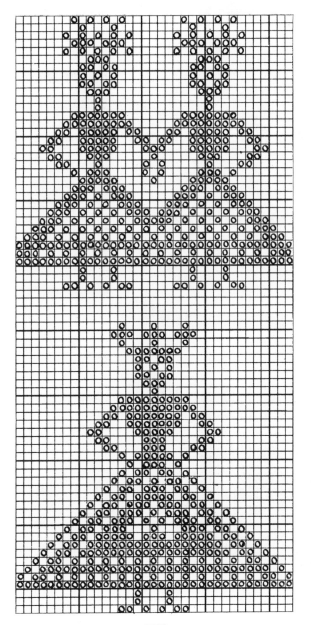

155

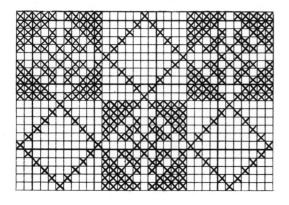

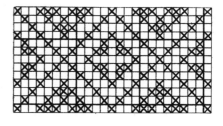

156

157

158

159

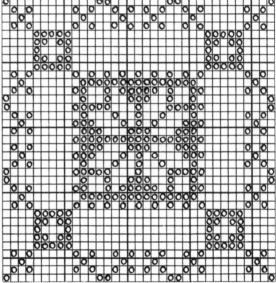

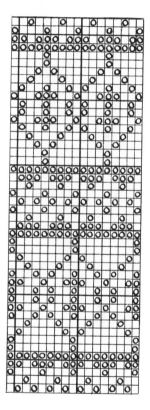

160

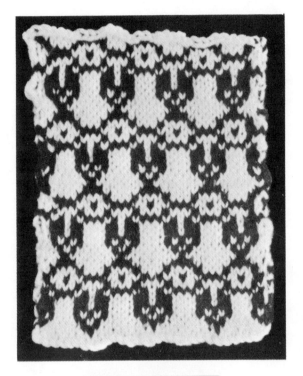

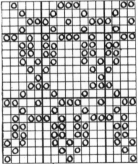

161

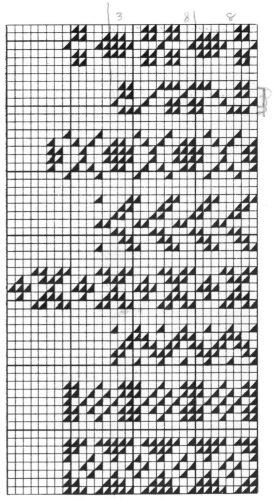

162

163

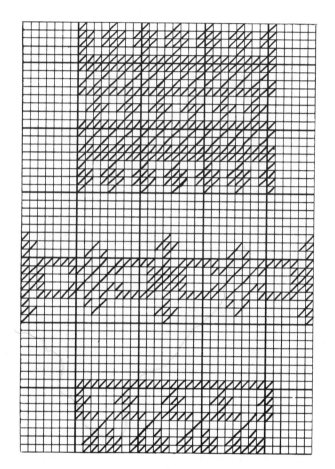

163

SCANDINAVIAN KNITTING PATTERNS
NORWEGIAN

Double Cable Pattern
Multiple of 14 + 2

164

1st row + P.2, K.12, rep. from + P.2.

2nd & every alt. row + K.2, P.12, rep. from + K.2.

3rd row + P.2, C.2B., K.8, rep. from + P.2.

5th row + P.2, K.4, C.4B., rep. from + P.2.

7th–14th rows Rep. 1–4 twice.

15th & 16th rows As 1st & 2nd.

17th row As 5th.

18th row + K.2, P.12, rep. from + K.2.

These 18 rows form the pattern

Twin Cable Pattern

Multiple of 11 + 2

165

1st row   + P.2, K.9, rep. from + P.2.

2nd & every alt. row   + K.2, P.4, K.1, P.4, rep. from + K.2.

3rd & 4th rows   As 1st & 2nd.

5th row   + P.2, C.2B., K.1, C.2F., rep. from + P.2.

6th row   + K.2, P.4, K.1, P.4, rep. from + K.2.

These 6 rows form the pattern

Ladder Cable Pattern

Multiple of 15 + 2

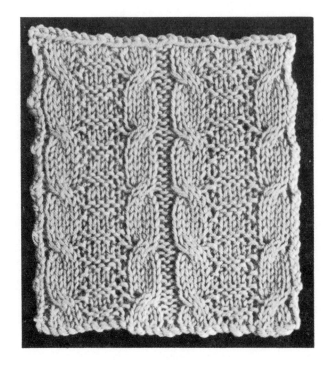

166

1st row + P.2, K.5, P.3, K.5, rep. from + P.2.

2nd row + K.2, P.4, K.5, P.4, rep. from + K.2.

3rd row + P.2, K.13, rep. from + P.2.

4th row + K.2, P.4, K.1, P.3, K.1, P.4, rep. from + K.2.

5th row + P.2, C.2B., K.1, P.3, K.1, C.2F., rep. from + P.2.

6th row As 2nd.

7th & 8th rows As 3rd & 4th.

These 8 rows form the pattern

Lace Cable Pattern

Multiple of 19 + 2

167

1st row + P.2, K.B.4, K.1, w.f., K.2 tog. t.b.l., K.3, K.2 tog., w.f., K.1, K.B.4, rep. from + P.2.

2nd, 4th & 6th rows + K.2, P.B.4, K.1, P.7, K.1, P.B.4, rep. from + K.2.

3rd row + P.2, K.B.4, K.2, w.f., K.2 tog. t.b.l., K.1, K.2 tog., w.f., K.2, K.B.4, rep. from + P.2.

5th row + P.2, CB.2F., K.3, w.f., sl.1, K.2 tog., p.s.s.o., w.f., K.3, CB.2B., rep. from + P.2.

7th row + P.2, K.B.4, K.9, K.B.4, rep. from + P.2.

8th row + K.2, P.B.4, K.1, P.7, K.1, P.B.4, rep. from + K.2.

These 8 rows form the pattern

SWEDISH

Chequer Pattern
Multiple of 4 + 2

168

1st row K.B. all across.	*5th & 6th rows* As 1st & 2nd.
2nd row P.B. all across.	*7th row* + P.2, K.B.2, rep. from + P.2.
3rd row + K.B.2, P.2, rep. from + K.B.2.	*8th row* + K.2, P.B.2, rep. from + K.2.
4th row + P.B.2, K.2, rep. from + P.B.2.	

These 8 rows form the pattern

Woven Pattern
Multiple of 2 + 1

Special Note. In working this pattern it is important that the Dark is carried loosely throughout the pattern.

Using Light cast on an odd number of sts. and P.1 row. Join in Dark.

169

1st row + K.1L., take D. to back in front of K. st., sl.1L., bring D. to front, rep. from + K.1L.

2nd row P.2L., carry D. across front of 2 sts. purled, + take D. to back, sl.1L., bring D. to front, P.1L., rep. from + P.1L.

These 2 rows form the pattern

Elongated Chequer Pattern
Multiple of 4 + 2

1st row + K.B.2, P.2, rep. from + K.B.2.

2nd row + P.B.2, K.2, rep. from + P.B.2.

3rd–6th rows Rep. 1st & 2nd twice.

7th row + P.2, K.B.2, rep. from + P.2.

8th row + K.2, P.B.2, rep. from + K.2.

9th & 10th rows As 7th & 8th.

11th & 12th rows As 1st & 2nd.

These 12 rows form the pattern

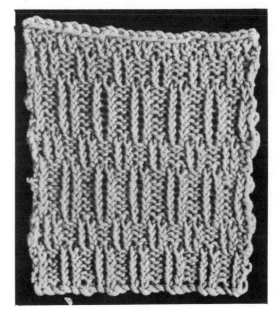

170

Square Pattern
Multiple of 6 + 2

1st row   + K.B.2, P.4, rep. from + K.B.2.

2nd row   + P.B.2, K.4, rep. from + P.B.2.

3rd row   + P.2, K.4, rep. from + P.2.

4th row   + K.2, P.4, rep. from + K.2.

5th–8th rows   Rep. 3rd & 4th twice.

These 8 rows form the pattern

171

DANISH

Pyramid Pattern
Multiple of 6 + 1

1st row   + K.1L., 5D., rep. from + 1L.

2nd row   + P.1L., 5D., rep. from + 1L.

3rd row   + K.2L., 3D., 1L., rep. from + 1L.

4th row   + P.2L., 3D., 1L., rep. from + 1L.

5th row   + K.3L., 1D., 2L., rep. from + 1L.

6th row   + P.3L., 1D., 2L., rep. from + 1L.

7th row   + K.2L., 1D., 1L., 1D., 1L., rep. from + 1L.

8th row   + P.3L., 1D., 2L., rep. from + 1L.

These 8 rows form the pattern

172

Chequer Pattern

Multiple of 8 + 5

1st row   + K.3D., 1L, 1D., 3L., rep. from + 3D., 1L., 1D.

2nd row   + P.2D., 1L., 2D., 3L., rep. from + 2D., 1L., 2D.

3rd row   + K.1D., 1L., 3D., 3L., rep. from + 1D., 1L., 3D.

4th row   + P.1D., 3L., 1D., 1L., 2D., rep. from + 1D., 3L., 1D.

5th row   + K.1D., 3L., 2D., 1L., 1D., rep. from + 1D., 3L., 1D.

6th row   + P.1D., 3L., 3D., 1L., rep. from + 1D., 3L., 1D.

These 6 rows form the pattern

173

Block Pattern

Multiple of 6 + 3

1st row   + K.3D., 3L., rep. from + 3D.

2nd row P.2D., 1L., + 2L., 3D., 1L., rep. from +.

3rd row   + K.2L., 3D., 1L., rep. from + 2L., 1D.

4th row P.1L., 2D., + 1D., 3L., 2D., rep. from +.

5th row   + K.2D., 3L., 1D., rep. from + 2D., 1L.

6th & 7th rows   As 4th & 5th.

8th row P.1D., 2L., + 1L., 3D., 2L., rep. from +.

9th row   + K.1L., 3D., 2L., rep. from + 1L., 2D.

10th row P.3D., + 3L., 3D., rep. from +.

11th row   + K.3L., 3D., rep. from + 3L.

12th row P.3L., + 3D., 3L., rep. from +.

13th & 14th rows   As 11th & 12th.

These 14 rows form the pattern

174

Broken Chequer Pattern

Multiple of 6 + 3

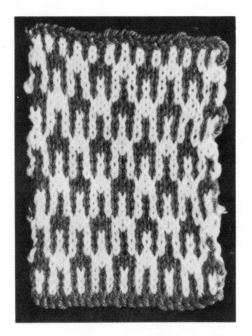

175

1st row + K.1D., 1L., rep. from + 1D.	*6th row* + P.1L., 1D., rep. from + 1L.
2nd row + P.1D., 1L., rep. from + 1D.	*7th row* + K.1L., 1D., rep. from + 1L.
3rd row As 1st.	*8th row* As 6th.
4th row + P.3D., 3L., rep. from + 3D.	*9th row* + K.3L., 3D., rep. from + 3L.
5th row + K.3D., 3L., rep. from + 3D.	*10th row* + P.3L., 3D., rep. from + 3L.

These 10 rows form the pattern

VII

Fair Isle and Shetland Knitting

FAIR ISLE knitting is certainly one of the most interesting examples of the craft in Europe today. It has certain characteristics that are peculiar to itself and although there is a tendency to call all forms of colour knitting 'Fair Isle Knitting', to do so is quite fallacious.

True Fair Isle patterns are Spanish in origin and in all of them we find a variation of the Armada Cross. No one knows exactly how these patterns reached Fair Isle from Spain, the current theory being that they were taken to Fair Isle by sailors of the Spanish Armada; or, if you like a more gruesome version of the theory, that the natives of Fair Isle copied the patterns from the clothing worn by the washed-up corpses that lay on the beaches round the island.

Although certain knitters in Shetland copy Fair Isle patterns, Shetland patterns themselves are definitely Norwegian in origin. Genuine Shetland patterning is always done in natural-coloured wools—white, cream, fawn, brown, grey and black. The wool is simply scoured and spun, no dyes of any kind being used. Nowadays Shetland wool can be purchased in the shops that has been dyed to match all the colours of the rainbow, but this is comparatively modern, lacking roots in the traditional story of knitting.

The hand knitters of the small island of Unst, the most northerly in Shetland, are world famous for their lace knitting. Their work is as fine as a cobweb, the wool being spun by hand, and in the most beautiful specimens being as fine as a human hair.

The Shetland lace tradition is not linked in any way with the earlier historical developments of the knitter's craft. Its origins are interesting. In the early years of the nineteenth century a Mrs. Jessie Scanlon visited Shetland, taking with her a collection of hand-made laces she had acquired during the Grand Tour. The Hunter family of Unst, who were very excited about these laces, developed a technique for copying them in hand knitting. The work of this family became world famous, and one of the earliest lace shawls they knitted was presented to Queen Victoria in the early years of her reign. The Hunter family have knitted shawls for the British Royal Family right up to the present time. The last of the Hunter family I met personally died a few years ago at the age of eighty-one, and in the collection of historical knitting owned by Patons & Baldwins Limited is the last shawl that Mrs. Hunter knitted; it is a museum piece, and is valued today at about £200.

Shetland lace patterns have never been written down, but have been handed down from one generation to another in an aural tradition that links these simple island people with the tradition that formed part of the background of craftsmanship before the printed work came into being.

The patterns themselves are built up from a series of simple lace stitches formed into diamonds, hexagonal shapes and lace stripes. The counterchange of patterns has led to an ever-changing variety of designs, so that no two shawls are ever identical, making each one as it is completed a unique contribution to the knitter's craft.

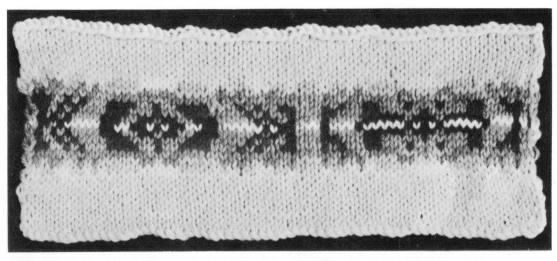

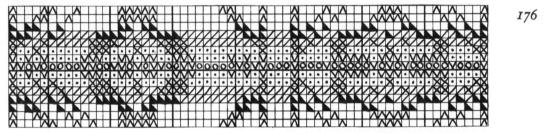

176

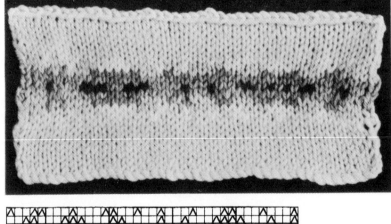

177

174

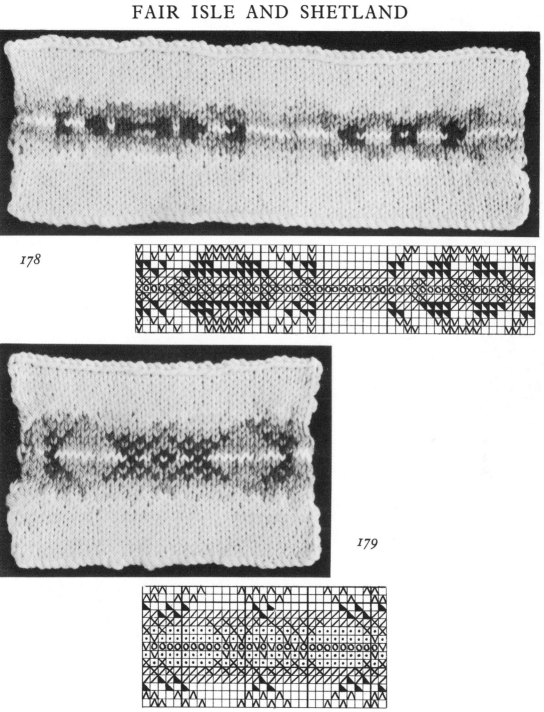

178

179

175

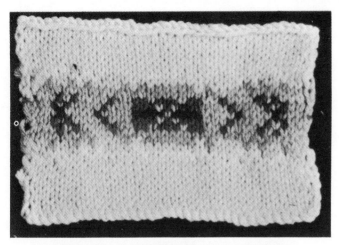

180

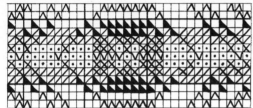

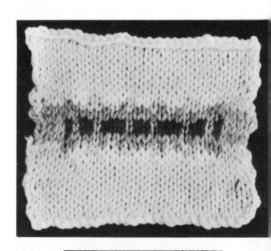

181

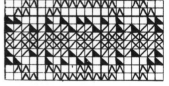

NOTE ON FAIR ISLE KNITTING

In Fair Isle Knitting the multi-coloured effect is obtained by changing the ground shade on one row and the contrast used on the pattern on the next, thus forming sequences of two rows in ground shade and two rows in pattern throughout up to the centre of the Chart.

For example:

In the 1st row a light shade is used for ground shade.

In the 2nd row the same ground shade is used and the 1st contrast introduced for pattern.

In the 3rd row the medium is used for ground shade, but the 1st contrast still used for the pattern.

In the 4th row medium is still used for the ground shade and the 2nd contrast for the pattern.

SHETLAND KNITTING PATTERNS

Old Shale Pattern

Multiple of 18 + 1

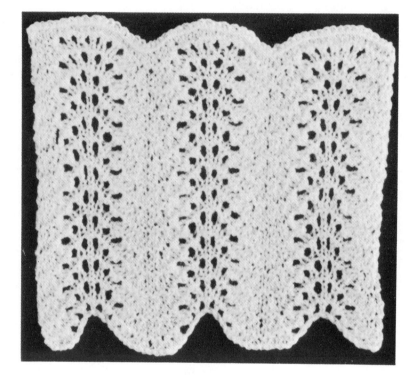

182

1st row   + K.1, (K.2 tog.) 3 times, (w.f., K.1) 5 times, w.f., (K.2 tog.) 3 times, rep. from + K.1.

2nd & 3rd rows   Knit.

4th row   Purl.

These 4 rows form the pattern.

This pattern is usually knitted in graduated stripes in the natural colours of Shetland Wool.

Shell Pattern

Multiple of 18 + 1

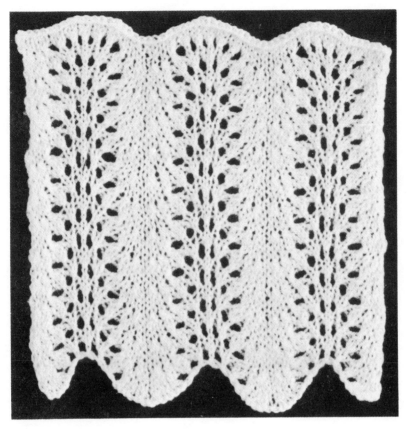

1st row + K.1, (K.2 tog.) **3** times, (w.f., K.1) 5 times, w.f., (K.2 tog. t.b.l.) **3** times, rep. from + K.1.

2nd row Purl.

3rd row Knit.

4th row Purl.

183

These 4 rows form the pattern

Crest of the Wave Pattern (see page 180)

Multiple of 12 + 1

1st & 2nd rows Knit.

3rd row Purl.

4th row Knit.

5th row + K.1, (K.2 tog.) twice, (w.f., K.1) 3 times, w.f., (K.2 tog. t.b.l.) twice, rep. from + K.1.

6th row Purl.

7th–12th rows Rep. 5th & 6th three times.

These 12 rows form the pattern

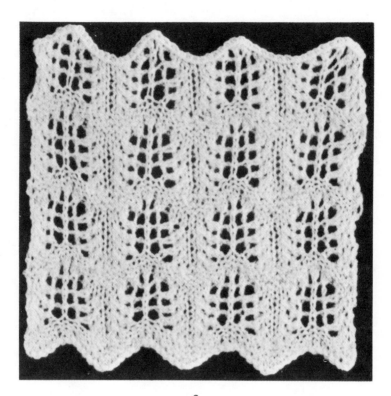

184

Feather and Fan Pattern   (*see page 181*)

Multiple of 14 + 1

1st row + K.1, K.4 tog., (w.f., K.1) 5 times, w.f., sl.2, K.2 tog., p.2.s.s.o., rep. from + K.1.

3rd row Knit.

2nd row + K.4, P.7, K.3, rep. from + K.1.

4th row Purl.

These 4 rows form the pattern

185

The following are the basic stitches used in Shetland lace knitting. I have given the principle of the patterns that I use to build up Shetland lace patterns as outlined at the beginning of this section.

Bead Stitch Pattern

Multiple of 9

186

1st row + K.2, K.2 tog., w.f., K.1, w.f., K.2 tog., K.2, rep. from +.

2nd row + K.1, K.2 tog., w.f., K.3, w.f., K.2 tog., K.1, rep. from +.

3rd row + K.2, w.f., K.2 tog., K.1, K.2 tog., w.f., K.2, rep. from +.

4th row + K.3, w.f., K.3 tog., w.f., K.3, rep. from +.

These 4 rows form the pattern

Madeira stitch—a fan-shaped openwork lace pattern worked against either a plain or a bead stitch background. The Madeiras can either be worked in simple fan formations, or more intricate groundings formed by ladder stitch formations worked into the Madeira motif.

Madeira and Ladder Pattern
Multiple of 13

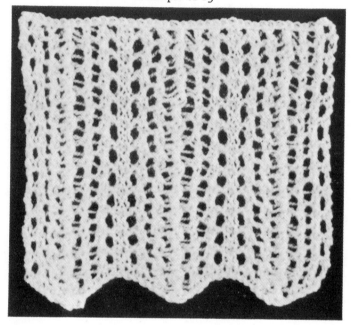

187

1st row + K.6, w.f., K.2 tog., K.5, rep. from +.

2nd row + K.5, w.f., K.3 tog., w.f., K.5, rep. from +.

3rd row + K.3, w.f., K.2 tog., w.f., K.3 tog., w.f., K.2 tog., w.f., K.3, rep. from +.

4th row + K.1, (w.f., K.2 tog.) twice, w.f., K.3 tog., (w.f., K.2 tog.) twice, w.f., K.1, rep. from +.

These 4 rows form the pattern

Cats Paw Pattern
Multiple of 11

1st row + K.3, K.2 tog., w.f., K.1, w.f., K.2 tog. t.b.l., K.3, rep. from +.

2nd & 4th rows Purl.

188

3rd row + K.2, K.2 tog., w.f., K.3, w.f., K.2 tog. t.b.l., K.2, rep. from +.

5th row + K.4, w.f., sl.1, K.2 tog., p.s.s.o., w.f., K.4, rep. from +.

6th row Purl.

These 6 rows form the pattern

Mrs. Hunter's Pattern

Multiple of 4 + 2

1st row Knit.

2nd row Purl.

3rd row K.1, + sl.1, K.3, p.s.s.o. 3 K. sts., rep. from + K.1.

4th row P.1, + P.3, w.r.n., rep. from + P.1.

These 4 rows form the pattern

189

Eyelet Pattern
Multiple of 15

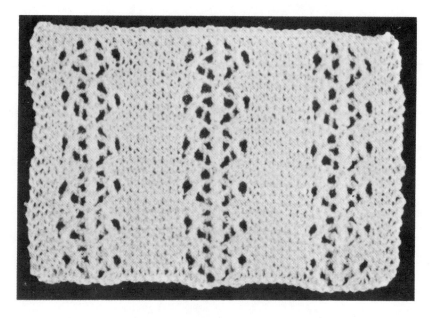

190

1st row + K.5, K.2 tog., w.f., K.1, w.f., K.2 tog., K.5, rep. from +.

2nd row + K.4, K.2 tog., w.f., K.3, w.f., K.2 tog., K.4, rep. from +.

3rd, 5th & 7th rows Knit.

4th row + K.4, w.f., K.2 tog., w.f., K.3 tog., w.f., K.2 tog., w.f., K.4, rep. from +.

6th row + K.6, w.f., K.3 tog., w.f., K.6, rep. from +.

8th row Knit.

A variation of this stitch is worked by repeating the first row twice and deleting the 8th row, there still being 8 rows to the pattern.

These 8 rows form the pattern

Fern Stitch Pattern
Multiple of 15

191

1st row + K.7, w.f., K.2 tog., K.6, rep. from +.

2nd, 4th, 6th, 8th & 10th rows Knit.

3rd row + K.5, K.2 tog., w.f., K.1, w.f., K.2 tog., K.5, rep. from +.

5th row + K.4, K.2 tog., w.f., K.3, w.f., K.2 tog., K.4, rep. from +.

7th row + K.4, w.f., K.2 tog., w.f., K.3 tog., w.f., K.2 tog., w.f., K.4, rep. from +.

9th row + K.2, K.2 tog., w.f., K.1, w.f., K.2 tog., K.1, K.2 tog., w.f., K.1, w.f., K.2 tog., K.2, rep. from +.

11th row + K.2, (w.f., K.2 tog.) twice, K.3, (K.2 tog., w.f.) twice, K.2, rep. from +.

12th row + K.3, w.f., K.2 tog., w.f., K.2 tog., K.1, K.2 tog., w.f., K.2 tog., w.f., K.3, rep. from +.

13th row + K.4, w.f., K.2 tog., w.f., K.3 tog., w.f., K.2 tog., w.f., K.4, rep. from +.

14th row + K.5, w.f., K.2 tog., K.1, K.2 tog., w.f., K.5, rep. from +.

15th row + K.6, w.f., K.3 tog., w.f., K.6, rep. from +

16th row Knit.

These 16 rows form the pattern

185

Lace Hole Pattern

Multiple of 12

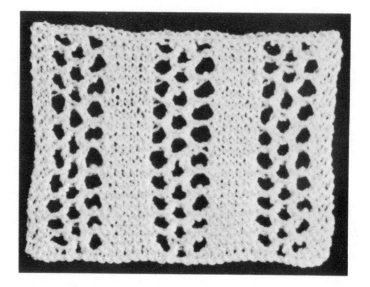

1st row + K.4, K.2 tog., (w.f.) twice, K.2 tog., K.4, rep. from +.

2nd row + K.5, (K.1, P.1) in w.f's of previous row, K.5, rep. from +.

3rd row + K.2, K.2 tog., (w.f.) twice, (K.2 tog.) twice, (w.f.) twice, K.2 tog., K.2, rep. from +.

4th row + K.3, (K.1, P.1) into w.f's of previous row, K.2, (P.1, K.1) into w.f's of previous row, K.3, rep. from +.

These 4 rows form the pattern

VIII

British Isles

THE BRITISH ISLES represents the richest tradition in knitting patterns that can be found in any part of the world.

The British are an island race who have been constantly subjected to invasions; one of the unique contributions made by Britain to the human story has been her ability to assimilate the various cultures she has come into contact with and re-create out of them her own heritage.

The Coptic Christians who founded the first British Church brought the knitting of the Nomads of North Africa. The Normans linked Britain with the developing culture of Europe.

The French gave bountifully of their lace stockings and the Italians of their Florentine knitted silk jackets. Later the men of Flanders came, establishing themselves as weavers. The Dutch merchants traded with Britain, part of their wares being the knitted stockings for which they were justly famous. The fishermen round the coastlines created their own patterns that they knitted in the Bridal Shirts, the traditional sweater of their port that they wore on their wedding day.

With the genius for assimilation Britain not only copied the traditional patterns from all these countries, but added to them her native genius, re-creating out of them patterns of her own.

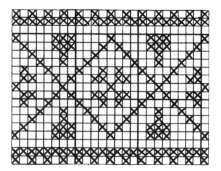

193

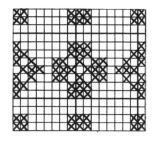

194

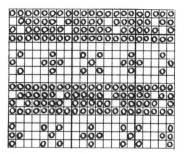

195

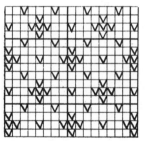

196

197

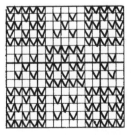

198

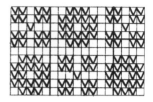

199

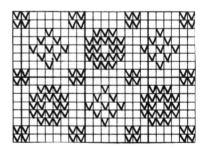

200

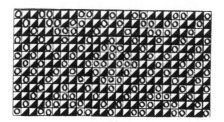

201

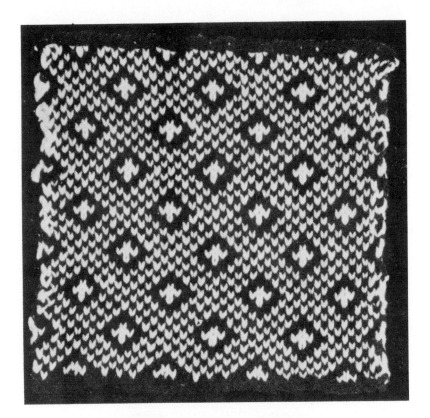

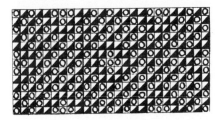

202

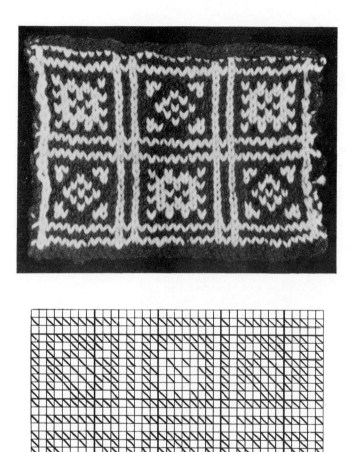

203

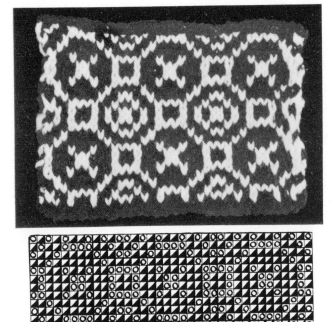

204

205

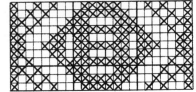

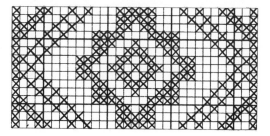

206

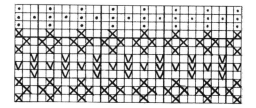

207

208

209

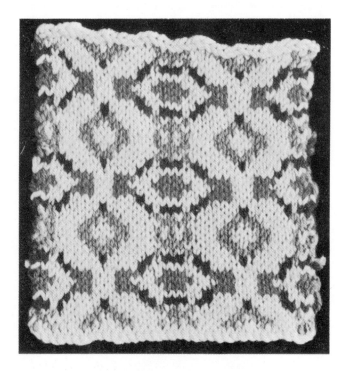

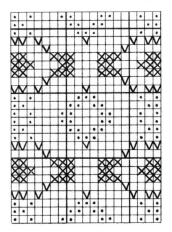

210

BRITISH ISLES

ENGLISH KNITTING PATTERNS

Diamond Quilting Pattern

Multiple of 6 + 2

1st row P.1, + w.r.n., P.5, w.r.n, P.1, rep. from + P.1.

2nd row K.1, + sl.1, drop w.r.n., K.4, sl.1, drop w.r.n., rep. from + K.1.

3rd row P.1, + sl.1, P.4, sl.1, rep. from + P.1.

4th row K.1, + sl.1, K.4. sl.1, rep. from + K.1.

5th row As 3rd.

6th row K.1, + drop next st., leave at front, K.2, pick up drop st. and K., sl.2, drop next st., sl.2 sl.sts. back on to left-hand needle, K. drop st., K.2, rep. from + K.1.

7th row P.1, + P.2, (w.r.n., P.1) twice, P.2, rep. from + P.1.

8th row K.1, + K.2, (sl.1, drop w.r.n.) twice, K.2, rep. from + K.1.

9th row P.1, + P.2, sl.2, P.2, rep. from + P.1.

10th row K.1, + K.2, sl.2, K.2, rep. from + K.1.

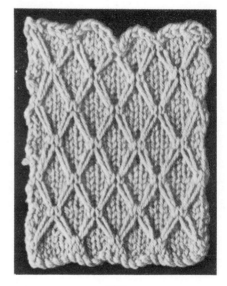

211

11th row As 9th.

12th row K.1, + sl.2, drop next st., leave at front, sl.2 back on needle, K. drop st., K.2, drop next st., K.2, K. drop st., rep. from + K.1.

These 12 rows form the pattern

Diamond Quilting Pattern (Two-colour Version)

Multiple of 6 + 2

1st row P.1G., w.r.n.C., P.1C., P.4G., w.r.n.C., P.1C., rep. from + P.1G.

2nd row Using G: K.1, + sl.1, drop w.r.n., K.4, sl.1, drop w.r.n., rep. from + K.1.

212

4th row Using G: K.1, + sl.1, K.4, sl.1, rep. from + K.1.

5th row As 3rd.

6th row K.1G., + drop next st., leave at front, K.2 G., pick up drop st., K. in C., sl. next 2 sts., drop next st., sl.2 back on needle, K. drop st. in C., K.2G., rep. from + K.1.

7th row P.1G., + P.2G., (w.r.n., P.1C.) twice, P.2G., rep. from + P.1.

8th row Using G: K.1, + K.2, (sl.1, drop w.r.n.) twice, K.2, rep. from + K.1.

9th row Using G: P.1, + P.2, sl.2, P.2, rep. from + P.1.

10th row Using G: K.1, + K.2, sl.2, K.2, rep. from + K.1.

11th row As 9th.

12th row K.1G., sl.2, drop next st., sl.2 back on needle, pick up drop st., K. in C., K.2G., drop next st., K.2G., pick up drop st., K. in C., rep. from + K.1.

3rd row Using G: P.1, + sl.1, P.4, sl.1, rep. from + P.1.

These 12 rows form the pattern

Hexagonal Quilting Pattern
Multiple of 6 + 2

1st row P.1, + P.2, (w.r.n., P.1) twice, P.2, rep. from + P.1.

2nd row K.1, + K.2, (sl.1, drop w.r.n.) twice, K.2, rep. from + K.1.

3rd row P.1, + P.2, sl.2, P.2, rep. from + P.1.

4th row K.1, + K.2, sl.2, K.2, rep. from + K.1.

5th row As 3rd.

6th row K.1, + sl.2, drop next st. at front, sl.2 back on needle, K. drop st., K.2, drop next st., K.2, K. drop st., rep. from + K.1.

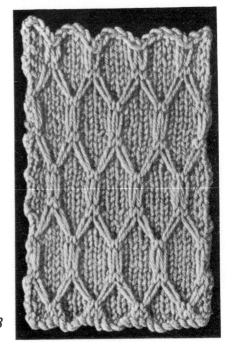

213

7th row P.1, + w.r.n., P.5, w.r.n., P.1, rep. from + P.1.

8th row K.1, + sl.1, drop w.r.n., K.4, sl.1, drop w.r.n., rep. from + K.1.

9th row P.1, + sl.1, P.4, sl.1, rep. from + P.1.

10th row K.1, + sl.1, K.4, sl.1, rep. from + K.1.

11th row As 9th.

12th row Knit.

13th row As 7th.

14th row As 8th.

15th row As 9th.

16th row As 10th.

17th row As 9th.

18th row K.1, + drop next st., leave at front, K.2, pick up drop st. and K., sl.2, drop next st., sl.2 sl. sts. back on to left-hand needle, K. drop st., K.2, rep. from + K.1.

19th row P.1, + P.2, (w.r.n., P.1) twice, P.2, rep. from + P.1.

20th row K.1, + K.2, (sl.1, drop w.r.n.) twice, K.2, rep. from + K.1.

21st row P.1, + P.2, sl.2, P.2, rep. from + P.1.

22nd row K.1, + K.2, sl.2, K.2, rep. from + K.1.

23rd row As 21st.

24th row Knit.

These 24 rows form the pattern

Quilted Travelling Leaf Pattern
Multiple of 10 + 1

1st row + K.1G., P.3G., w.r.n.C., P.2C., P.4G., rep. from + K.1G.

2nd row + K.5G., K.1C., sl. next st., drop w.r.n., K.3G., rep. from + K.1G.

3rd row + K.1G., P.3G., sl.1, P.1C., w.r.n., P.1C., P.3G., rep. from + K.1G.

4th row + K.4G., sl.1, drop w.r.n., K.1C., drop next st., leave at front, K.2G., pick up drop st. K. in G., K.1G., rep. from + K.1G.

5th row + K.1G., P.3G., w.r.n.C., P.2C., sl.1, P.3G., rep. from + K.1G.

6th row + K.2G., sl.2, drop next st. and leave at front, sl.2 back on needle, K. drop st. G., K.2G., K.1C., sl.1, drop w.r.n., K.3G., rep. from + K.1G.

The 3rd to 6th rows form the pattern

214

Basket Weave Pattern

Multiple of 4 + 2

1st row   Knit.

2nd row   K.1, P. to last st., K.1.

3rd row   K.2, + P.2, K.2, rep. from +.

4th row   K.1, P.1, + K.2, P.2, rep. from + P.1, K.1.

5th & 6th rows   Rep. 1st & 2nd.

7th row   K.1, P.1, + K.2, P.2, rep. from + P.1, K.1.

8th row   K.2, + P.2, K.2, rep. from +.

These 8 rows form the pattern

215

Dewdrop Pattern

Multiple of 6 + 1

216

1st row   K.2 tog., w.f., + K.3, w.f., sl.1, K.2 tog., p.s.s.o., w.f., rep. from + K.3, w.f., K.2 tog.

2nd row   K.2, + P.3, K.3, rep. from + P.3, K.2.

3rd row   P.2, + K.3, P.3, rep. from + K.3, P.2.

4th row   As 2nd.

5th row   K.2, + w.f., sl.1, K.2 tog., p.s.s.o., w.f., K.3, rep. from + w.f., sl.1, K.2 tog., p.s.s.o., w.f., K.2.

These 8 rows form the pattern

Lattice Pattern
Multiple of 8 + 2

1st row   K.1, + C.4F., rep. from + K.1.

2nd row   Purl.

3rd row   Knit.

4th row   Purl.

5th row   K.5, + C.4B., rep. from + K.5.

6th, 7th & 8th rows   As 2nd, 3rd & 4th.

These 8 rows form the pattern

217

Acorn Pattern
Multiple of 10 + 2

1st row   K.1, P.3, K.4, + P.6, K.4, rep. from + P.3, K.1.

2nd row   K.4, P.4, + K.6, P.4, rep. from + K.4.

3rd row   K.1, P.1, + Cr.A by slipping next 2 sts. on to spare needle, leave at back, K.2, P.2, from spare needle, (K.1, P.1) into thread connecting 2 sts. of previous row, Cr.B by slipping next 2 sts. on to spare needle, leave at front, P.2, K.2, from spare needle, P.2, rep. from + P.1, K.1.

4th row   K.2, + P.2, K.2, rep. from +.

5th row   K.1, P.1, + K.2, P.2, rep. from + K.2, P.1, K.1.

6th row   As 4th.

7th row   K.2, + sl.1, K.1, p.s.s.o., P.6, K.2 tog., K.2, rep. from +.

203

218

8th row   K.1, P.2, K.6, + P.4, K.6, rep. from + P.2, K.1.

9th row   K.1, K. once into thread of previous row + Cr.B., P.2, Cr.A, (K.1, P.1) into thread of previous row, rep. from + K.1 into thread of previous row, K.1.

10th row   K.1, P.1, + K.2, P.2, rep. from + K.2, P.1, K.1.

11th row   K.2, + P.2, K.2, rep. from +.

12th row   As 10th.

13th row   K.1, P.3, + K.2 tog., K.2, sl.1, K.1, p.s.s.o., P.6, rep. from + K.2 tog., K.2, sl.1, K.1, p.s.s.o., P.3, K.1.

Rep. from 2nd to 13th rows incl.

Blackberry Pattern
Multiple of 16 + 15

1st row   (Wrong side) + P.3, K.1, P.3, cast on 4, P. cast on sts., P.4, K.1, P.3, K.1, rep. from + P.3, K.1, P.3, cast on 4, P. cast on sts., P.4, K.1, P.3.

2nd row   + K.3, P.1, K.11, P.1, K.3, P.1, rep. from + K.3, P.1, K.11, P.1, K.3.

3rd row   + P.3, K.1, P.2, cast on 4, P. cast on sts., P.1, P.5 tog., cast on 4, P. cast on sts., P.3, K.1, P.3, K.1, rep. from + P.3, K.1, P.2, cast on 4, P. cast on sts., P.1, P.5 tog., cast on 4, P. cast on sts., P.3, K.1, P.3.

4th row   + K.3, P.1, K.15, P.1, K.3, P.1, rep. from + K.3, P.1, K.15, P.1, K.3.

5th row   + P.3, K.1, P.1, (cast on 4, P. cast on sts., P.1, P.5 tog.) twice, cast on 4, P. cast on sts., P.2, K.1, P.3, K.1, rep. from + P.3, K.1, P.1, (cast on 4, P. cast on sts., P.1, P.5 tog.) twice, cast on 4, P. cast on sts., P.2, K.1, P.3.

6th row   + K.3, P.1, K.19, P.1, K.3, P.1, rep. from + K.3, P.1, K.19, P.1, K.3.

219

7th row + P.3, K.1, (P.1, P.5 tog.) 3 times, P.1, K.1, P.3, cast on 4, P. cast on sts., K.1, rep. from + P.3, K.1, (P.1, P.5 tog.) 3 times, P.1, K.1, P.3.

8th row + (K.3, P.1) 3 times, K.8, rep. from + (K.3, P.1) 3 times, K.3.

9th row P.3, + (K.1, P.3) twice, K.1, P.2, cast on 4, P. cast on sts., P.1, P.5 tog., cast on 4, P. cast on sts., P.3, rep. from + (K.1, P.3) 3 times.

10th row K.3, + (P.1, K.3) twice, P.1, K.15, rep. from + (P.1, K.3) 3 times.

11th row P.3, + (K.1, P.3) twice, K.1, P.1, (cast on 4, P. cast on sts., P.1, P.5 tog.) twice, cast on 4, P. cast on sts., P.2, rep. from + (K.1, P.3) 3 times.

12th row K.3, + (P.1, K.3) twice, P.1, K.19, rep. from + (P.1, K.3) 3 times.

13th row P.3, + K.1, P.3, cast on 4, P. cast on sts., K.1, P.3, K.1, (P.1, P.5 tog.) 3 times, P.1, rep. from + K.1, P.3, cast on 4, P. cast on sts., K.1, P.3, K.1, P.3.

Rows 2–13 incl. complete the pattern when first pattern has been done.

Dotted Chevron Pattern

Multiple of 20 + 1

220

1st row K.1, + w.f., sl.1, K.1, p.s.s.o., K.15, K.2 tog., w.f., K.1, rep. from +.

2nd row K.1, P.1, + w.r.n., P.2 tog., P.13, P.2 tog., w.r.n., P.3, rep. from + w.r.n., P.2 tog., P.13, P.2 tog., w.r.n., P.1, K.1.

3rd row K.3, + w.f., sl.1, K.1, p.s.s.o., K.11, K.2 tog., w.f., K.5, rep. from + w.f., sl.1, K.1, p.s.s.o., K.11, K.2 tog., w.f., K.3.

4th row K.1, P.3, + w.r.n., P.2 tog., P.9, P.2 tog., w.r.n., P.7, rep. from + w.r.n., P.2 tog., P.9, P.2 tog., w.r.n., P.3, K.1.

5th row K.5, + w.f., sl.1, K.1, p.s.s.o., K.3,

Make Bobble thus: K.1, P.1, K.1, P1, K.1 into next st., turn, K.5, turn, cast off 4, K.3, K.2 tog., w.f., K.9, rep. from + w.f., sl.1, K.1, p.s.s.o., K.3, Make Bobble, K3, K2 tog., w.f., K.5.

6th row K.1, P.5, + w.r.n., P.2 tog., P.5, P.2 tog., w.r.n., P.11, rep. from + w.r.n., P.2 tog., P.5, P.2 tog., w.r.n., P.5, K.1.

7th row K.7, + w.f., sl.1, K.1, p.s.s.o., K.3, K.2 tog., w.f., K.6, Make Bobble, K.6, rep. from + w.f., sl.1, K.1, p.s.s.o., K.3, K.2 tog., w.f., K.7.

8th row K.1, P.7, + w.r.n., P.2 tog., P.1, P.2 tog., w.r.n., P.15, rep. from + w.r.n., P.2 tog., P.1, P.2 tog., w.r.n., P.7, K.1.

9th row K.9, + w.f., sl.1, K.2 tog., p.s.s.o., w.f., K.17, rep. from + w.f., sl.1, K.2 tog., p.s.s.o., w.f., K.9.

10th row K.1, P. to last st., K.1.

These 10 rows form the pattern

Club Stitch Pattern
Multiple of 13 + 2

221

1st row K.1, w.f., + K.2 tog., (P.3, K.5 into next st.) twice, P.3, w.o.n., rep. from + K.2 tog., (P.3, K.5 into next st.) twice, P.3, K.1.

2nd row K.1, + (K.3, P.5) twice, K.3, w.f., K.2 tog., rep. from + K.1.

3rd row K.1, w.f., + K.2 tog., (P.3, K.5) twice, P.3, w.o.n., rep. from + K.2 tog., (P.3, K.5) twice, P.3, K.1.

4th row As 2nd.

5th row As 3rd.

6th row As 2nd.

7th row K.1, w.f., + K.2 tog., P.3, (sl.1, K.1, p.s.s.o., K.1, K.2 tog., P.3) twice, w.o.n., rep. from + K.2 tog., P.3, (sl.1, K.1, p.s.s.o., K.1, K.2 tog., P.3) twice, K.1.

8th row K.1, + (K.3, P.3) twice, K.3, w.f., K.2 tog., rep. from + K.1.

207

9th row   K.1, w.f., + K.2 tog., P.3, (sl.1, K.2 tog., p.s.s.o., P.3) twice, w.o.n., rep. from + K.2 tog., P.3, (sl.1, K.2 tog., p.s.s.o., P.3) twice, K.1.

10th row   K.1, + (K.3, P.1) twice, K.3, w.f., K.2 tog., rep. from + K.1.

11th row   K.1, w.f., + K.2 tog., (P.3, K.5 into next st.) twice, P.3, w.o.n., rep. from + K.2 tog., (P.3, K.5 into next st.) twice, K.1.

12th row   K.1, + (K.3, P.5 tog.,) twice, K.3, w.f., K.2 tog., rep. from + K.1.

13th row   K.1, w.f., + K.2 tog., P.11, w.o.n., rep. from + K.2 tog., P.11, K.1.

14th row   K.1, + K.11, w.f., K.2 tog., rep. from + K.1.

These 14 rows form the pattern

Diamond Block Pattern

Multiple of 14 + 2

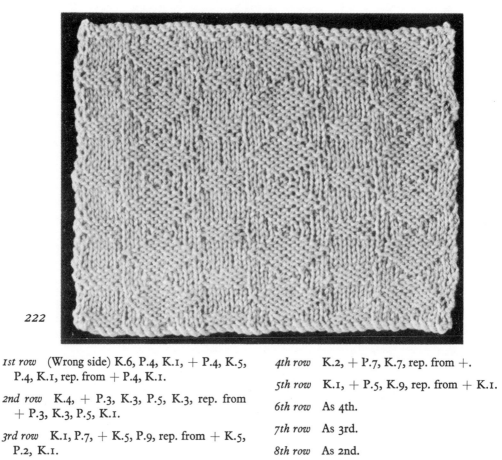

222

1st row   (Wrong side) K.6, P.4, K.1, + P.4, K.5, P.4, K.1, rep. from + P.4, K.1.

2nd row   K.4, + P.3, K.3, P.5, K.3, rep. from + P.3, K.3, P.5, K.1.

3rd row   K.1, P.7, + K.5, P.9, rep. from + K.5, P.2, K.1.

4th row   K.2, + P.7, K.7, rep. from +.

5th row   K.1, + P.5, K.9, rep. from + K.1.

6th row   As 4th.

7th row   As 3rd.

8th row   As 2nd.

These 8 rows form the pattern

Lacy Diamond Pattern

Multiple of 12 + 1

223

1st row P.1, + K.2 tog., K.3, w.f., K.1, w.f., K.3, K.2 tog. t.b.l., P.1, rep. from +.

2nd, 4th, 6th & 8th rows K.1, + P.11, K.1, rep. from +.

3rd row P.1, + K.2 tog., K.2, w.f., K.3, w.f., K.2, K.2 tog. t.b.l., P.1, rep. from +.

5th row P.1, + K.2 tog., K.1, w.f., K.5, w.f., K.1, K.2 tog. t.b.l., P.1, rep. from +.

7th row P.1, + K.2 tog., w.f., K.7, w.f., K.2 tog. t.b.l., P.1, rep. from +.

9th row K.1, + w.f., K.3, K.2 tog. t.b.l., P.1, K.2 tog., K.3, w.f., K.1, rep. from +.

10th, 12th & 14th rows P.6, K.1, + P.11, K.1, rep. from + P.6.

11th row K.2, + w.f., K.2, K.2 tog. t.b.l., P.1, K.2 tog., K.2, w.f., K.3, rep. from + w.f., K.2, K.2 tog. t.b.l., P.1, K.2 tog., K.2, w.f., K.2.

13th row K.3, + w.f., K.1, K.2 tog. t.b.l., P.1, K.2 tog., K.1, w.f., K.5, rep. from + w.f., K.1, K.2 tog. t.b.l., P.1, K.2 tog., K.1, w.f., K.3.

15th row K.4, + w.f., K.2 tog. t.b.l., P.1, K.2 tog., w.f., K.7, rep. from + w.f., K.2 tog. t.b.l., P.1, K.2 tog., w.f., K.4.

16th row As 10th.

These 16 rows form the pattern

Fern Stitch Pattern

Multiple of 12

1st row   K.5, + K.2 tog., w.f., K.1, w.f., sl.1, K.1, p.s.s.o., K.7, rep. from + K.2 tog., w.f., K.5.

2nd & every alt. row   K.1, P. to last st., K.1.

3rd row   K.4, + K.2 tog., K.1, w.f., K.1, w.f., K.1, sl.1, K.1, p.s.s.o., K.5, rep. from + K.2 tog., K.1, w.f., K.5.

5th row   K.3, + K.2 tog., K.2, w.f., K.1, w.f., K.2, sl.1, K.1, p.s.s.o., K.3, rep. from + K.2 tog., K.2, w.f., K.5.

7th row   K.2, + K.2 tog., K.3, w.f., K.1, w.f., K.3, sl.1, K.1, p.s.s.o., K.1, rep. from + K.2 tog., K.3, w.f., K.5.

9th row   K.1, K.2 tog., + K.4, w.f., K.1, w.f., K.4, sl.1, K.2 tog., p.s.s.o., rep. from + K.4, w.f., K.5.

11th row   K.2, + w.f., sl.1, K.1, p.s.s.o., K.7, K.2 tog., w.f., K.1, rep. from + w.f., sl.1, K.1, p.s.s.o., K.8.

13th row   K.2, + w.f., K.1, sl.1, K.1, p.s.s.o., K.5, K.2 tog., K.1, w.f., K.1, rep. from + w.f., K.1, sl.1, K.1, p.s.s.o., K.7.

15th row   K.2, + w.f., K.2, sl.1, K.1, p.s.s.o., K.3, K.2 tog., K.2, w.f., K.1, rep. from + w.f., K.2, sl.1, K.1, p.s.s.o., K.6.

17th row   K.2, + w.f., K.3, sl.1, K.1, p.s.s.o., K.1, K.2 tog., K.3, w.f., K.1, rep. from + w.f., K.3, sl.1, K.1, p.s.s.o., K.5.

19th row   K.2, + w.f., K.4, sl.1, K.2 tog., p.s.s.o., K.4, w.f., K.1, rep. from + w.f., K.4, sl.1, K.1, p.s.s.o., K.4.

20th row   K.1, P. to last st., K.1.

These 20 rows form the pattern

Mock Kilting Pattern
Multiple of 9

225

1st row	+ K.8, P.1, rep. from +.		*5th row*	+ K.4, P.5, rep. from +.
2nd row	+ K.2, P.7, rep. from +.		*6th row*	+ K.6, P.3, rep. from +.
3rd row	+ K.6, P.3, rep. from +.		*7th row*	+ K.2, P.7, rep. from +.
4th row	+ K.4, P.5, rep. from +.		*8th row*	+ K.8, P.1, rep. from +.

These 8 rows form the pattern

Rib Pattern (see page 212)
Multiple of 4

1st row	+ K.B.1, K.2, P.1, rep. from +.		*4th row*	+ K.2, P.1, P.B.1, rep. from +.
2nd row	+ K.1, P.2, P.B.1, rep. from +.		*5th row*	+ K.B.1, P.3, rep. from +.
3rd row	+ K.B.1, K.1, P.2, rep. from +.		*6th row*	+ K.3, P.B.1, rep. from +.

These 6 rows form the pattern

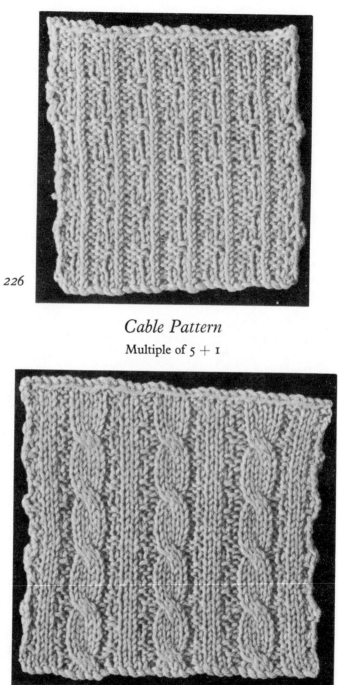

226

Cable Pattern

Multiple of 5 + 1

227

1st row + P.1, K.4, rep. from + P.1.
2nd row + K.1, P.4, rep. from + K.1.

3rd row + P.2, K.2, P.2, C.2F., rep. from + P.2, K.2, P.2.

4th row   + K.2, P.2, K.2, P.4, rep. from + K.2, P.2, K.2.

5th & 6th rows   As 1st & 2nd.

7th row   + P.2, K.2, P.2, K.4, rep. from + P.2, K.2, P.2.

8th row   + K.2, P.2, K.2, P.4, rep. from + K.2, P.2, K.2.

These 8 rows form the pattern

Seeded Rib Pattern
Multiple of 12 + 2

228

1st row   + K.2, P.10, rep. from + K.2.

2nd row   + P.2, (K.1, P.3, K.1) twice, rep. from + P.2.

3rd row   + K.2, (P.2, K.1, P.2) twice, rep. from + K.2.

4th row   + P.2, K.10, rep. from + P.2.

These 4 rows form the pattern

Bubble Rib Pattern   *(see page 214)*
Multiple of 4 + 2

1st row   K.B. all across.

2nd row   P.B. all across.

3rd row   + K.B.2, P.2, rep. from + K.B.2.

4th row   + P.B.2, K.2, rep. from + P.B.2.

These 4 rows form the pattern

213

229

Chequer Pattern
Multiple of 4 + 2

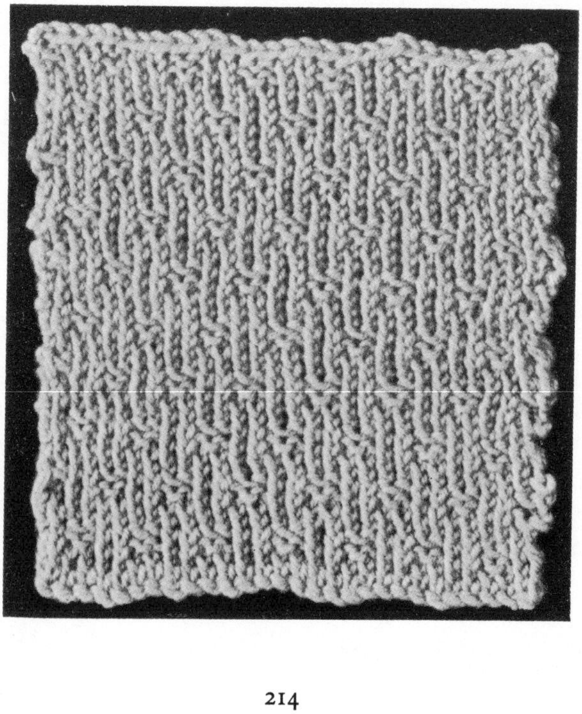

230

1st row K.B. all across.	*5th row* K.B. all across.
2nd row P.B. all across.	*6th row* P.B. all across.
3rd row + K.B.2, P.2, rep. from + K.B.2.	*7th row* + P.2, K.B.2, rep. from + P.2.
4th row + P.B.2, K.2, rep. from + P.B.2.	*8th row* + K.2, P.B.2, rep. from + K.2.

These 8 rows form the pattern

Mock Tartan Pattern

Multiple of 16 + 1

(Special Note: The colours in this pattern are picked out from Scottish Tartans, a ground shade and four contrasting colours being used.)

231

1st row Using G: P.1, K.7, rep. from + P.1.	*3rd–10th rows* Rep. 1st & 2nd four times.
2nd row Using G: Purl.	*11th & 12th rows* Using 1st C: As 1st & 2nd.

215

(When knitting is completed, work a chain st. in crochet using 3rd contrast up 1st and every alternate purl st. ridge. Complete by working chain st. up remaining P. st. ridges in 4th contrast.)

These 16 rows form the pattern

Sanquar Pattern No. 1

Multiple of 18

(This pattern has become world famous and is used for gloves and stockings. Two colours are used, brown and natural or dark grey and white, being the traditional colours used for these patterns.)

232

1st row   + K.9D., 9L., rep. from +.

2nd row   + P.9L., 1D., 2L., 1D., 1L., 1D., 2L., 1D., rep. from +.

3rd row   + (K.1D., 1L) 4 times, 1D., 9L., rep. from +.

4th row   + P.9L., 2D., 1L., 3D., 1L., 2D., rep. from +.

5th row + K.1.D, 1L., (2D., 1L.) twice, 1D., 9L., rep. from +.

6th–9th rows Rep. 4th, 3rd, 2nd & 1st.

10th–18th rows Reading Purl for Knit and Knit for Purl throughout work as rows 1–9, thus interchanging patt. block for self colour block throughout.

Sanquar Pattern No. 2

Multiple of 18

233

1st row + K.9D., 9L., rep. from +.

2nd row + P.9L., 9D., rep. from +.

3rd row + K.2D., 2L., 1D., 2L., 2D., 9L., rep. from +.

4th row + P.9L., 2D., 1L., 3D., 1L., 2D., rep. from +.

5th row + K.9D., 9L., rep. from +.

6th–9th rows Rep. 4th, 3rd, 2nd & 1st.

10th–18th rows Reading Purl for Knit and Knit for Purl throughout work as rows 1–9, thus interchanging patt. block for self colour block throughout.

Sanquar Pattern No. 3

Multiple of 18

234

1st row + K.1L., 7D., 10L., rep. from +.

2nd row + P.9L., 3D., 3L., 3D., rep. from +.

3rd row + K.2D., 2L., 1D., 2L., 2D., 9L., rep. from +.

4th row + P.9L., (1D., 3L) twice, 1D., rep. from +.

5th row + K.1D., 1L., (2D., 1L.) twice, 1D., 9L., rep. from +.

6th–9th rows Rep. 4th, 3rd, 2nd & 1st.

10th–18th rows Reading Purl for Knit and Knit for Purl throughout work as rows 1–9, thus interchanging patt. block for self colour block throughout.

Moss Stitch Rib Pattern

Multiple of 11 + 2

235

1st row   + Tw.2, K.1, P.1, K.1, Tw.3, K.1, P.1, K.1, rep. from + Tw. 2.

2nd row   + P.2, K.1, P.1, K.1, P.3, K.1, P.1, K.1, rep. from + P.2.

3rd row   + Tw.2, K.1, P.1, K.5, P.1, K1, rep. from + Tw.2.

4th row   As 2nd.

These 4 rows form the pattern

Arrow Rib Pattern

Multiple of 14 + 3

1st row   (Wrong side) + P.4, K.3, P.3, K.3, P.1, rep. from + P.3.

2nd row   + Tw.3, Cr.P.1F. by slipping next st. on cable needle leave at front, P.1, K. st. from cable needle, P.2, Tw.3, P.2, Cr.P.1B. by slipping next st. on cable needle leave at back, K.1, P. st. from cable needle, rep. from + Tw.3.

3rd row + P.3, K.1, P.1, K.2, P.3, K.2, P.1, K.1, rep. from + P.3.

4th row + K.3, P.1, Cr.P.1F., P.1, K3, P.1, Cr.P.1B., P.1, rep. from + K.3.

5th row + P.3, K.2, P.1, K.1, P.3, K.1, P.1, K.2, rep. from + P.3.

6th row + Tw.3, P.2, Cr.P.1F., Tw.3, Cr.P.1B., P.2, rep. from + Tw.3.

7th row + P.3, K.3, P.5, K.3, rep. from + P.3.

8th row + K.3, P.4, rep. from + K.3.

These 8 rows form the pattern

236

Twisted Basket Pattern

Multiple of 8 + 3

237

1st row + P.5, Tw.3, rep. from + P.5.

2nd row + K.5, P.3, rep. from + K.5.

3rd & 4th rows As 1st & 2nd.

5th row P.1, + Tw.3, P.5, rep. from + Tw.3, P.1.

6th row K.1, + P.3, K.5, rep. from + P.3, K.1.

7th & 8th rows As 5th & 6th.

These 8 rows form the pattern

Twisted Chequer Pattern

Multiple of 4 + 2

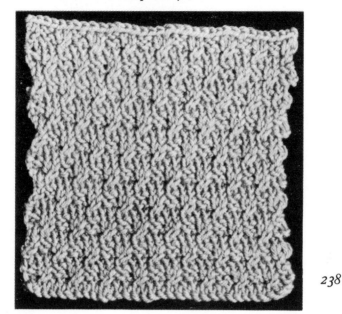

238

1st row K.B. all across.	*5th & 6th rows* As 1st & 2nd.
2nd row P.B. all across.	
3rd row + P.2, Tw.2, rep. from + P.2.	*7th row* + Tw.2, P.2, rep. from + Tw.2.
4th row + K.2, P.2, rep. from + K.2.	*8th row* + P.2, K.2, rep. from + P.2.

These 8 rows form the pattern

Herringbone Pattern

Multiple of 6 + 1

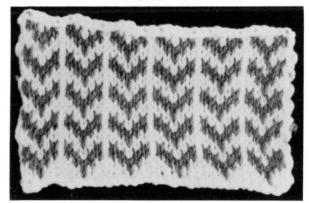

239

1st row   + K.B.1L., K.2L., 1D., 2L., rep. from + K.B.1L.

2nd row   + P.B.1L., P.1L., 3D., 1L., rep. from + P.B.1L.

3rd row   + K.B.1L., K.2D., 1L., 2D., rep. from + K.B.1L.

4th row   + P.B.1L., P.1D., 3L., 1D., rep. from + P.B.1L.

These 4 rows form the pattern

Wave and Seed Pattern
Multiple of 8 + 1

240

1st row   + K.4L., 1D., 3L., rep. from + 1L.

2nd row   + P.3L., 3D., 2L., rep. from + 1L.

3rd row   + K.2L., 2D., 1L., 2D., 1L., rep. from + 1L.

4th row   + P.1L., 2D., 3L., 2D., rep. from + 1L.

5th row   + K.2D., 2L., 1D., 2L., 1D., rep. from + 1D.

6th row   + P.1D., 2L., 3D., 2L., rep. from + 1D.

7th row   As 1st.

8th row   Using L: Purl.

These 8 rows form the pattern

Tweed Striped Pattern

Multiple of 8

1st row + K.3L., 4D., 1L., rep. from +.

2nd row + P.1D., 1L., 2D., 1L., 1D., 2L., rep. from +.

3rd row + K.1L., 1D., 2L., 1D., 1L., 2D., rep. from +.

4th row + P.3D., 4L., 1D., rep. from +.

These 4 rows form the pattern

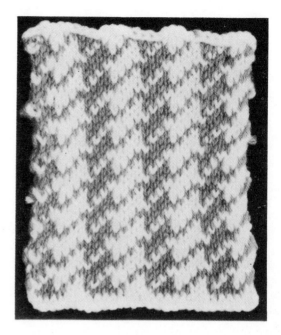

241

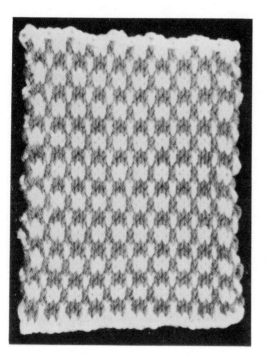

Striped Ladder Pattern

Multiple of 3 + 1

1st row + K.B.1L., K.2D., rep. from + K.B.1L.

2nd row + P.B.1L., P.2D., rep. from + P.B.1L.

3rd row + K.B.1D., K.2L., rep. from + K.B.1D.

4th row + P.B.1D., P.2L., rep. from + P.B.1D.

These 4 rows form the pattern

242

NOTE ON USE OF CHARTS FOR FISHERMEN'S SWEATER PATTERNS

In reading the charts, the odd rows are knit rows and the even rows purl rows; the dots on the knit rows being purled and on the purl rows being knitted throughout.

The large circles represent the cable movement that is worked across the number of stitches within the circle, thus if we have 8 stitches it will be a cable 4 movement, 10 stitches a cable 5 movement, etc.

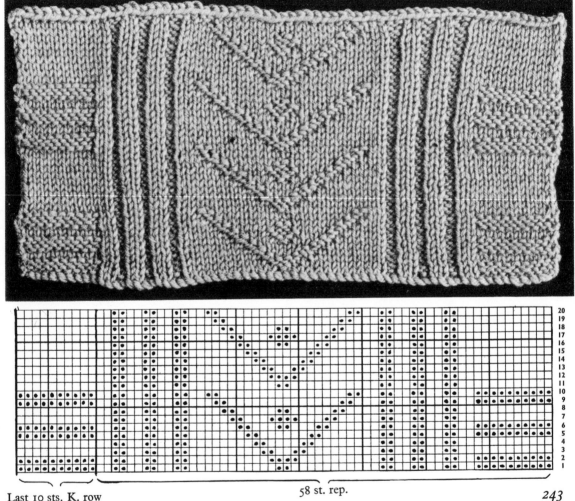

Last 10 sts. K. row
First 10 sts. P. row

58 st. rep.

243

PORT: INVERNESS

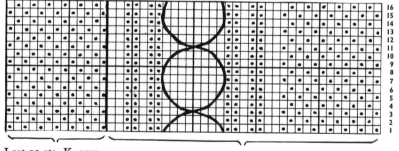

Last 13 sts. K. row
First 13 sts. P. row

35 st. rep.

244

PORT: BANFF

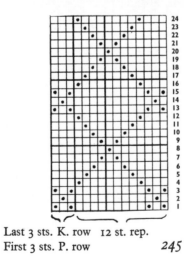

Last 3 sts. K. row   12 st. rep.
First 3 sts. P. row   *245*

PORT: NOT SPECIFIC, COMMON TO MANY

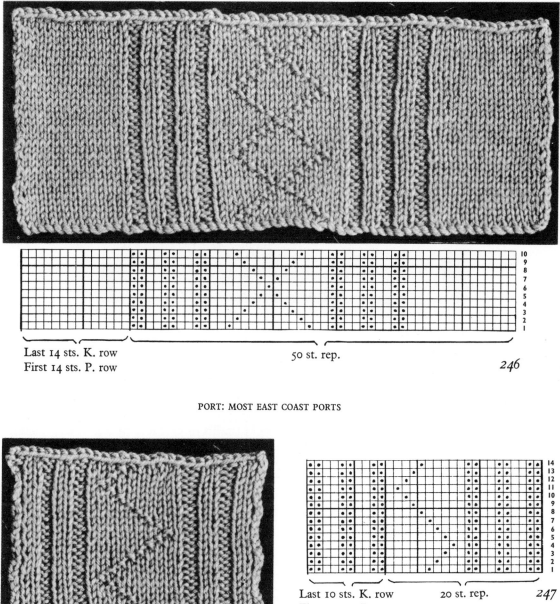

Last 14 sts. K. row
First 14 sts. P. row

50 st. rep.

246

PORT: MOST EAST COAST PORTS

Last 10 sts. K. row
First 10 sts. P. row

20 st. rep.

247

PORT: LERWICK

227

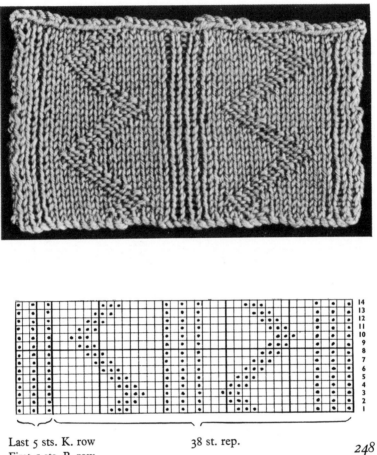

Last 5 sts. K. row
First 5 sts. P. row

38 st. rep.

248

PORT: WICK

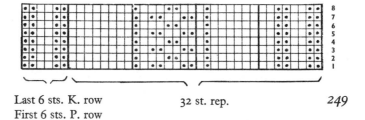

Last 6 sts. K. row
First 6 sts. P. row
32 st. rep.
249

PORT: NAIRN

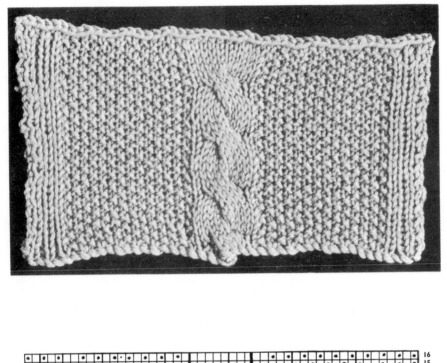

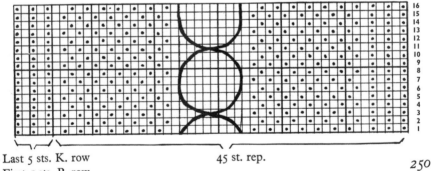

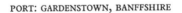

Last 5 sts. K. row   45 st. rep.
First 5 sts. P. row   *250*

PORT: GARDENSTOWN, BANFFSHIRE

FISHERMEN'S SWEATERS

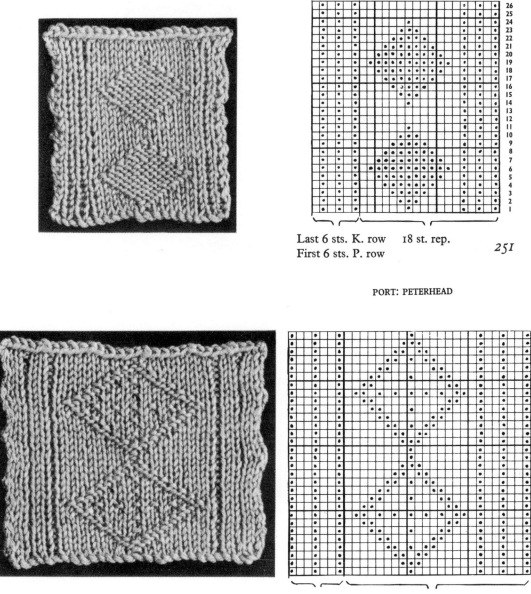

Last 6 sts. K. row   18 st. rep.
First 6 sts. P. row

251

PORT: PETERHEAD

Last 7 sts. K. row   24 st. rep.
First 7 sts. P. row

252

PORT: CRUDEN BAY, PETERHEAD AREA

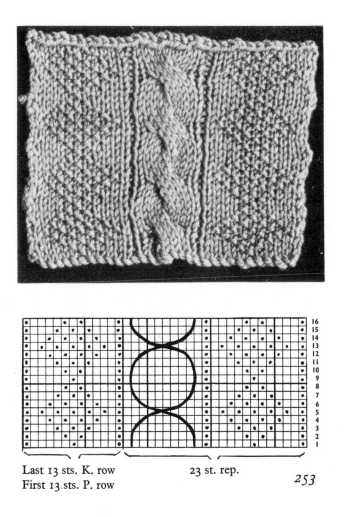

Last 13 sts. K. row
First 13 sts. P. row

23 st. rep.

253

PORT: BUCKIE

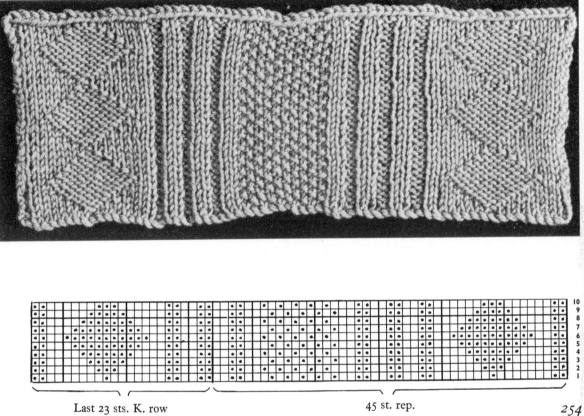

Last 23 sts. K. row
First 23 sts. P. row

45 st. rep.

254

PORT: CULLEN

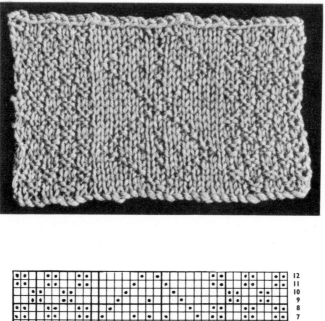

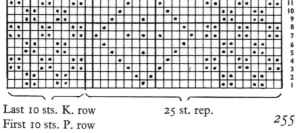

Last 10 sts. K. row   25 st. rep.
First 10 sts. P. row   *255*

PORT: NAIRN AREA

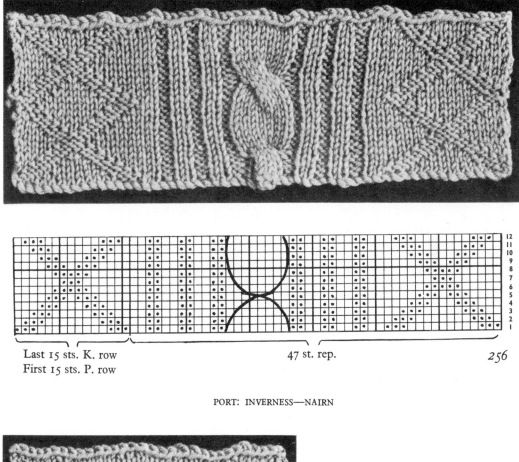

Last 15 sts. K. row
First 15 sts. P. row

47 st. rep.

256

PORT: INVERNESS—NAIRN

257

PORT: KIRKCALDY—FIFE COASTS

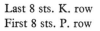

Last 8 sts. K. row
First 8 sts. P. row

24 st. rep.

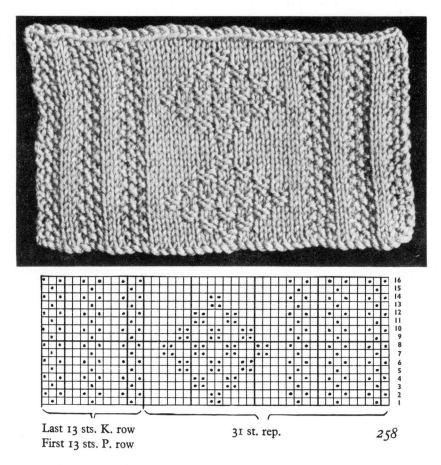

Last 13 sts. K. row
First 13 sts. P. row

31 st. rep.

258

PORT: BANFF—PORT KNOCKIE—PORTSOY

Last 4 sts. K. row 8 st. rep. 259
First 4 sts. P. row

PORT: COMMON, MAINLY
TO SOUTH AS ST. MONANCE
AND KIRKCALDY

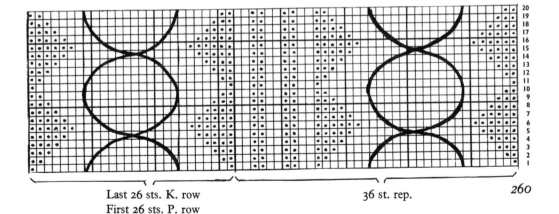

Last 26 sts. K. row
First 26 sts. P. row

36 st. rep.

260

PORT: INVERNESS AREA

261

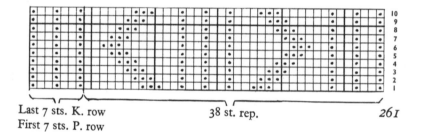

Last 7 sts. K. row   38 st. rep.   *261*
First 7 sts. P. row

PORT: LERWICK OR WICK

262

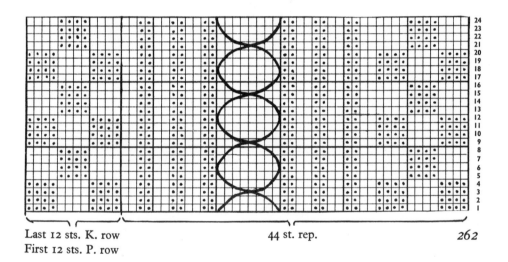

Last 12 sts. K. row
First 12 sts. P. row

44 st. rep.

262

PORT: COMMON SOUTH OF INVERNESS

263

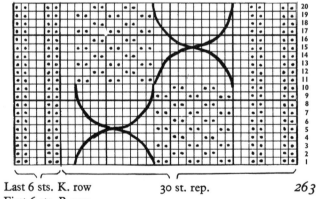

Last 6 sts. K. row   30 st. rep.   *263*
First 6 sts. P. row

PORT: PETERHEAD

A CATALOGUE OF SELECTED DOVER BOOKS
IN ALL FIELDS OF INTEREST

THE NOTEBOOKS OF LEONARDO DA VINCI, edited by J.P. Richter. Extracts from manuscripts reveal great genius; on painting, sculpture, anatomy, sciences, geography, etc. Both Italian and English. 186 ms. pages reproduced, plus 500 additional drawings, including studies for Last Supper, Sforza monument, etc. 860pp. 7⅞ x 10¾.   USO 22572-0, 22573-9 Pa., Two vol. set $15.90

ART NOUVEAU DESIGNS IN COLOR, Alphonse Mucha, Maurice Verneuil, Georges Auriol. Full-color reproduction of Combinaisons ornamentales (c. 1900) by Art Nouveau masters. Floral, animal, geometric, interlacings, swashes — borders, frames, spots — all incredibly beautiful. 60 plates, hundreds of designs. 9⅜ x 8¹/₁₆ .   22885-1 Pa. $4.00

GRAPHIC WORKS OF ODILON REDON. All great fantastic lithographs, etchings, engravings, drawings, 209 in all. Monsters, Huysmans, still life work, etc. Introduction by Alfred Werner. 209pp. 9⅛ x 12¼.   21996-8 Pa. $6.00

EXOTIC FLORAL PATTERNS IN COLOR, E.-A. Seguy. Incredibly beautiful full-color pochoir work by great French designer of 20's. Complete Bouquets et frondaisons, Suggestions pour étoffes. Richness must be seen to be believed. 40 plates containing 120 patterns. 80pp. 9⅜ x 12¼.   23041-4 Pa. $6.00

SELECTED ETCHINGS OF JAMES A. McN. WHISTLER, James A. McN. Whistler. 149 outstanding etchings by the great American artist, including selections from the Thames set and two Venice sets, the complete French set, and many individual prints. Introduction and explanatory note on each print by Maria Naylor. 157pp. 9⅜ x 12¼.   23194-1 Pa. $5.00

VISUAL ILLUSIONS: THEIR CAUSES, CHARACTERISTICS, AND APPLICATIONS, Matthew Luckiesh. Thorough description, discussion; shape and size, color, motion; natural illusion. Uses in art and industry. 100 illustrations. 252pp.
                                                   21530-X Pa. $2.50

TEN BOOKS ON ARCHITECTURE, Vitruvius. The most important book ever written on architecture. Early Roman aesthetics, technology, classical orders, site selection, all other aspects. Stands behind everything since. Morgan translation. 331pp.
                                                   20645-9 Pa. $3.50

THE CODEX NUTTALL. A PICTURE MANUSCRIPT FROM ANCIENT MEXICO, as first edited by Zelia Nuttall. Only inexpensive edition, in full color, of a pre-Columbian Mexican (Mixtec) book. 88 color plates show kings, gods, heroes, temples, sacrifices. New explanatory, historical introduction by Arthur G. Miller. 96pp. 11⅜ x 8½.   23168-2 Pa. $7.50

JEWISH GREETING CARDS, Ed Sibbett, Jr. 16 cards to cut and color. Three say "Happy Chanukah," one "Happy New Year," others have no message, show stars of David, Torahs, wine cups, other traditional themes. 16 envelopes. 8¼ x 11.
23225-5 Pa. $2.00

AUBREY BEARDSLEY GREETING CARD BOOK, Aubrey Beardsley. Edited by Theodore Menten. 16 elegant yet inexpensive greeting cards let you combine your own sentiments with subtle Art Nouveau lines. 16 different Aubrey Beardsley designs that you can color or not, as you wish. 16 envelopes. 64pp. 8¼ x 11.
23173-9 Pa. $2.00

RECREATIONS IN THE THEORY OF NUMBERS, Albert Beiler. Number theory, an inexhaustible source of puzzles, recreations, for beginners and advanced. Divisors, perfect numbers. scales of notation, etc. 349pp. 21096-0 Pa. $4.00

AMUSEMENTS IN MATHEMATICS, Henry E. Dudeney. One of largest puzzle collections, based on algebra, arithmetic, permutations, probability, plane figure dissection, properties of numbers, by one of world's foremost puzzlists. Solutions. 450 illustrations. 258pp. 20473-1 Pa. $3.00

MATHEMATICS, MAGIC AND MYSTERY, Martin Gardner. Puzzle editor for Scientific American explains math behind: card tricks, stage mind reading, coin and match tricks, counting out games, geometric dissections. Probability, sets, theory of numbers, clearly explained. Plus more than 400 tricks, guaranteed to work. 135 illustrations. 176pp. 20335-2 Pa. $2.00

BEST MATHEMATICAL PUZZLES OF SAM LOYD, edited by Martin Gardner. Bizarre, original, whimsical puzzles by America's greatest puzzler. From fabulously rare Cyclopedia, including famous 14-15 puzzles, the Horse of a Different Color, 115 more. Elementary math. 150 illustrations. 167pp. 20498-7 Pa. $2.50

MATHEMATICAL PUZZLES FOR BEGINNERS AND ENTHUSIASTS, Geoffrey Mott-Smith. 189 puzzles from easy to difficult involving arithmetic, logic, algebra, properties of digits, probability. Explanation of math behind puzzles. 135 illustrations. 248pp. 20198-8 Pa. $2.75

BIG BOOK OF MAZES AND LABYRINTHS, Walter Shepherd. Classical, solid, and ripple mazes; short path and avoidance labyrinths; more — 50 mazes and labyrinths in all. 12 other figures. Full solutions. 112pp. 8⅛ x 11. 22951-3 Pa. $2.00

COIN GAMES AND PUZZLES, Maxey Brooke. 60 puzzles, games and stunts — from Japan, Korea, Africa and the ancient world, by Dudeney and the other great puzzlers, as well as Maxey Brooke's own creations. Full solutions. 67 illustrations. 94pp. 22893-2 Pa. $1.50

HAND SHADOWS TO BE THROWN UPON THE WALL, Henry Bursill. Wonderful Victorian novelty tells how to make flying birds, dog, goose, deer, and 14 others. 32pp. 6½ x 9¼. 21779-5 Pa. $1.25

DECORATIVE ALPHABETS AND INITIALS, edited by Alexander Nesbitt. 91 complete alphabets (medieval to modern), 3924 decorative initials, including Victorian novelty and Art Nouveau. 192pp. 7¾ x 10¾.   20544-4 Pa. $4.00

CALLIGRAPHY, Arthur Baker. Over 100 original alphabets from the hand of our greatest living calligrapher: simple, bold, fine-line, richly ornamented, etc. — all strikingly original and different, a fusion of many influences and styles. 155pp. 11⅜ x 8¼.   22895-9 Pa. $4.50

MONOGRAMS AND ALPHABETIC DEVICES, edited by Hayward and Blanche Cirker. Over 2500 combinations, names, crests in very varied styles: script engraving, ornate Victorian, simple Roman, and many others. 226pp. 8⅛ x 11.

22330-2 Pa. $5.00

THE BOOK OF SIGNS, Rudolf Koch. Famed German type designer renders 493 symbols: religious, alchemical, imperial, runes, property marks, etc. Timeless. 104pp. 6⅛ x 9¼.   20162-7 Pa. $1.75

200 DECORATIVE TITLE PAGES, edited by Alexander Nesbitt. 1478 to late 1920's. Baskerville, Dürer, Beardsley, W. Morris, Pyle, many others in most varied techniques. For posters, programs, other uses. 222pp. 8⅜ x 11¼.   21264-5 Pa. **$5.00**

DICTIONARY OF AMERICAN PORTRAITS, edited by Hayward and Blanche Cirker. 4000 important Americans, earliest times to 1905, mostly in clear line. Politicians, writers, soldiers, scientists, inventors, industrialists, Indians, Blacks, women, outlaws, etc. Identificatory information. 756pp. 9¼ x 12¾. 21823-6 Clothbd. $30.00

ART FORMS IN NATURE, Ernst Haeckel. Multitude of strangely beautiful natural forms: Radiolaria, Foraminifera, jellyfishes, fungi, turtles, bats, etc. All 100 plates of the 19th century evolutionist's Kunstformen der Natur (1904). 100pp. 9⅜ x 12¼.   22987-4 Pa. $4.00

DECOUPAGE: THE BIG PICTURE SOURCEBOOK, Eleanor Rawlings. Make hundreds of beautiful objects, over 550 florals, animals, letters, shells, period costumes, frames, etc. selected by foremost practitioner. Printed on one side of page. 8 color plates. Instructions. 176pp. 9³/₁₆ x 12¼.   23182-8 Pa. $5.00

AMERICAN FOLK DECORATION, Jean Lipman, Eve Meulendyke. Thorough coverage of all aspects of wood, tin, leather, paper, cloth decoration — scapes, humans, trees, flowers, geometrics — and how to make them. Full instructions. 233 illustrations, 5 in color. 163pp. 8⅜ x 11¼.   22217-9 Pa. $3.95

WHITTLING AND WOODCARVING, E.J. Tangerman. Best book on market; clear, full. If you can cut a potato, you can carve toys, puzzles, chains, caricatures, masks, patterns, frames, decorate surfaces, etc. Also covers serious wood sculpture. Over 200 photos. 293pp.   20965-2 Pa. $3.00

THE ART DECO STYLE, ed. by Theodore Menten. Furniture, jewelry, metalwork, ceramics, fabrics, lighting fixtures, interior decors, exteriors, graphics from pure French sources. Best sampling around. Over 400 photographs. 183pp. 8⅜ x 11¼.
22824-X Pa. $4.00

THE GENTLEMAN AND CABINET MAKER'S DIRECTOR, Thomas Chippendale. Full reprint, 1762 style book, most influential of all time; chairs, tables, sofas, mirrors, cabinets, etc. 200 plates, plus 24 photographs of surviving pieces. 249pp. 9⅞ x 12¾.
21601-2 Pa. $6.00

PINE FURNITURE OF EARLY NEW ENGLAND, Russell H. Kettell. Basic book. Thorough historical text, plus 200 illustrations of boxes, highboys, candlesticks, desks, etc. 477pp. 7⅞ x 10¾.
20145-7 Clothbd. $12.50

ORIENTAL RUGS, ANTIQUE AND MODERN, Walter A. Hawley. Persia, Turkey, Caucasus, Central Asia, China, other traditions. Best general survey of all aspects: styles and periods, manufacture, uses, symbols and their interpretation, and identification. 96 illustrations, 11 in color. 320pp. 6⅛ x 9¼.
22366-3 Pa. $5.00

DECORATIVE ANTIQUE IRONWORK, Henry R. d'Allemagne. Photographs of 4500 iron artifacts from world's finest collection, Rouen. Hinges, locks, candelabra, weapons, lighting devices, clocks, tools, from Roman times to mid-19th century. Nothing else comparable to it. 420pp. 9 x 12.
22082-6 Pa. $8.50

THE COMPLETE BOOK OF DOLL MAKING AND COLLECTING, Catherine Christopher. Instructions, patterns for dozens of dolls, from rag doll on up to elaborate, historically accurate figures. Mould faces, sew clothing, make doll houses, etc. Also collecting information. Many illustrations. 288pp. 6 x 9. 22066-4 Pa. $3.00

ANTIQUE PAPER DOLLS: 1915-1920, edited by Arnold Arnold. 7 antique cut-out dolls and 24 costumes from 1915-1920, selected by Arnold Arnold from his collection of rare children's books and entertainments, all in full color. 32pp. 9¼ x 12¼.
23176-3 Pa. $2.00

ANTIQUE PAPER DOLLS: THE EDWARDIAN ERA, Epinal. Full-color reproductions of two historic series of paper dolls that show clothing styles in 1908 and at the beginning of the First World War. 8 two-sided, stand-up dolls and 32 complete, two-sided costumes. Full instructions for assembling included. 32pp. 9¼ x 12¼.
23175-5 Pa. $2.00

A HISTORY OF COSTUME, Carl Köhler, Emma von Sichardt. Egypt, Babylon, Greece up through 19th century Europe; based on surviving pieces, art works, etc. Full text and 595 illustrations, including many clear, measured patterns for reproducing historic costume. Practical. 464pp.
21030-8 Pa. $4.00

EARLY AMERICAN LOCOMOTIVES, John H. White, Jr. Finest locomotive engravings from late 19th century: historical (1804-1874), main-line (after 1870), special, foreign, etc. 147 plates. 200pp. 11⅜ x 8¼.
22772-3 Pa. $3.50

150 MASTERPIECES OF DRAWING, edited by Anthony Toney. 150 plates, early 15th century to end of 18th century; Rembrandt, Michelangelo, Dürer, Fragonard, Watteau, Wouwerman, many others. 150pp. 8⅜ x 11¼. 21032-4 Pa. $4.00

THE GOLDEN AGE OF THE POSTER, Hayward and Blanche Cirker. 70 extraordinary posters in full colors, from Maîtres de l'Affiche, Mucha, Lautrec, Bradley, Cheret, Beardsley, many others. 9⅜ x 12¼. 22753-7 Pa. $4.95
21718-3 Clothbd. $7.95

SIMPLICISSIMUS, selection, translations and text by Stanley Appelbaum. 180 satirical drawings, 16 in full color, from the famous German weekly magazine in the years 1896 to 1926. 24 artists included: Grosz, Kley, Pascin, Kubin, Kollwitz, plus Heine, Thöny, Bruno Paul, others. 172pp. 8½ x 12¼. 23098-8 Pa. $5.00
23099-6 Clothbd. $10.00

THE EARLY WORK OF AUBREY BEARDSLEY, Aubrey Beardsley. 157 plates, 2 in color: Manon Lescaut, Madame Bovary, Morte d'Arthur, Salome, other. Introduction by H. Marillier. 175pp. 8½ x 11. 21816-3 Pa. $4.00

THE LATER WORK OF AUBREY BEARDSLEY, Aubrey Beardsley. Exotic masterpieces of full maturity: Venus and Tannhäuser, Lysistrata, Rape of the Lock, Volpone, Savoy material, etc. 174 plates, 2 in color. 176pp. 8½ x 11. 21817-1 Pa. $4.00

DRAWINGS OF WILLIAM BLAKE, William Blake. 92 plates from Book of Job, Divine Comedy, Paradise Lost, visionary heads, mythological figures, Laocoön, etc. Selection, introduction, commentary by Sir Geoffrey Keynes. 178pp. 8½ x 11. 22303-5 Pa. $3.50

LONDON: A PILGRIMAGE, Gustave Doré, Blanchard Jerrold. Squalor, riches, misery, beauty of mid-Victorian metropolis; 55 wonderful plates, 125 other illustrations, full social, cultural text by Jerrold. 191pp. of text. 8⅛ x 11. 22306-X Pa. $5.00

THE COMPLETE WOODCUTS OF ALBRECHT DÜRER, edited by Dr. W. Kurth. 346 in all: Old Testament, St. Jerome, Passion, Life of Virgin, Apocalypse, many others. Introduction by Campbell Dodgson. 285pp. 8½ x 12¼. 21097-9 Pa. $6.00

THE DISASTERS OF WAR, Francisco Goya. 83 etchings record horrors of Napoleonic wars in Spain and war in general. Reprint of 1st edition, plus 3 additional plates. Introduction by Philip Hofer. 97pp. 9⅜ x 8¼. 21872-4 Pa. $3.00

ENGRAVINGS OF HOGARTH, William Hogarth. 101 of Hogarth's greatest works: Rake's Progress, Harlot's Progress, Illustrations for Hudibras, Midnight Modern Conversation, Before and After, Beer Street and Gin Lane, many more. Full commentary. 256pp. 11 x 14. 22479-1 Pa. $7.00
23023-6 Clothbd. $13.50

PRIMITIVE ART, Franz Boas. Great anthropologist on ceramics, textiles, wood, stone, metal, etc.; patterns, technology, symbols, styles. All areas, but fullest on Northwest Coast Indians. 350 illustrations. 378pp. 20025-6 Pa. $3.75

AUSTRIAN COOKING AND BAKING, Gretel Beer. Authentic thick soups, wiener schnitzel, veal goulash, more, plus dumplings, puff pastries, nut cakes, sacher tortes, other great Austrian desserts. 224pp. USO 23220-4 Pa. $2.50

CHEESES OF THE WORLD, U.S.D.A. Dictionary of cheeses containing descriptions of over 400 varieties of cheese from common Cheddar to exotic Surati. Up to two pages are given to important cheeses like Camembert, Cottage, Edam, etc. 151pp. 22831-2 Pa. $1.50

TRITTON'S GUIDE TO BETTER WINE AND BEER MAKING FOR BEGINNERS, S.M. Tritton. All you need to know to make family-sized quantities of over 100 types of grape, fruit, herb, vegetable wines; plus beers, mead, cider, more. 11 illustrations. 157pp. USO 22528-3 Pa. $2.25

DECORATIVE LABELS FOR HOME CANNING, PRESERVING, AND OTHER HOUSEHOLD AND GIFT USES, Theodore Menten. 128 gummed, perforated labels, beautifully printed in 2 colors. 12 versions in traditional, Art Nouveau, Art Deco styles. Adhere to metal, glass, wood, most plastics. 24pp. 8¼ x 11. 23219-0 Pa. $2.00

FIVE ACRES AND INDEPENDENCE, Maurice G. Kains. Great back-to-the-land classic explains basics of self-sufficient farming: economics, plants, crops, animals, orchards, soils, land selection, host of other necessary things. Do not confuse with skimpy faddist literature; Kains was one of America's greatest agriculturalists. 95 illustrations. 397pp. 20974-1 Pa. $3.00

GROWING VEGETABLES IN THE HOME GARDEN, U.S. Dept. of Agriculture. Basic information on site, soil conditions, selection of vegetables, planting, cultivation, gathering. Up-to-date, concise, authoritative. Covers 60 vegetables. 30 illustrations. 123pp. 23167-4 Pa. $1.35

FRUITS FOR THE HOME GARDEN, Dr. U.P. Hedrick. A chapter covering each type of garden fruit, advice on plant care, soils, grafting, pruning, sprays, transplanting, and much more! Very full. 53 illustrations. 175pp. 22944-0 Pa. $2.50

GARDENING ON SANDY SOIL IN NORTH TEMPERATE AREAS, Christine Kelway. Is your soil too light, too sandy? Improve your soil, select plants that survive under such conditions. Both vegetables and flowers. 42 photos. 148pp.
USO 23199-2 Pa. $2.50

THE FRAGRANT GARDEN: A BOOK ABOUT SWEET SCENTED FLOWERS AND LEAVES, Louise Beebe Wilder. Fullest, best book on growing plants for their fragrances. Descriptions of hundreds of plants, both well-known and overlooked. 407pp.
23071-6 Pa. $4.00

EASY GARDENING WITH DROUGHT-RESISTANT PLANTS, Arno and Irene Nehrling. Authoritative guide to gardening with plants that require a minimum of water: seashore, desert, and rock gardens; house plants; annuals and perennials; much more. 190 illustrations. 320pp. 23230-1 Pa. $3.50

CATALOGUE OF DOVER BOOKS

THE MAGIC MOVING PICTURE BOOK, Bliss, Sands & Co. The pictures in this book move! Volcanoes erupt, a house burns, a serpentine dancer wiggles her way through a number. By using a specially ruled acetate screen provided, you can obtain these and 15 other startling effects. Originally "The Motograph Moving Picture Book." 32pp. 8¼ x 11.   23224-7 Pa. $1.75

STRING FIGURES AND HOW TO MAKE THEM, Caroline F. Jayne. Fullest, clearest instructions on string figures from around world: Eskimo, Navajo, Lapp, Europe, more. Cats cradle, moving spear, lightning, stars. Introduction by A.C. Haddon. 950 illustrations. 407pp.   20152-X Pa. $3.50

PAPER FOLDING FOR BEGINNERS, William D. Murray and Francis J. Rigney. Clearest book on market for making origami sail boats, roosters, frogs that move legs, cups, bonbon boxes. 40 projects. More than 275 illustrations. Photographs. 94pp.
20713-7 Pa. $1.25

INDIAN SIGN LANGUAGE, William Tomkins. Over 525 signs developed by Sioux, Blackfoot, Cheyenne, Arapahoe and other tribes. Written instructions and diagrams: how to make words, construct sentences. Also 290 pictographs of Sioux and Ojibway tribes. 111pp. 6⅛ x 9¼.   22029-X Pa. $1.50

BOOMERANGS: HOW TO MAKE AND THROW THEM, Bernard S. Mason. Easy to make and throw, dozens of designs: cross-stick, pinwheel, boomabird, tumblestick, Australian curved stick boomerang. Complete throwing instructions. All safe. 99pp.   23028-7 Pa. $1.75

25 KITES THAT FLY, Leslie Hunt. Full, easy to follow instructions for kites made from inexpensive materials. Many novelties. Reeling, raising, designing your own. 70 illustrations. 110pp.   22550-X Pa. $1.25

TRICKS AND GAMES ON THE POOL TABLE, Fred Herrmann. 79 tricks and games, some solitaires, some for 2 or more players, some competitive; mystifying shots and throws, unusual carom, tricks involving cork, coins, a hat, more. 77 figures. 95pp.   21814-7 Pa. $1.25

WOODCRAFT AND CAMPING, Bernard S. Mason. How to make a quick emergency shelter, select woods that will burn immediately, make do with limited supplies, etc. Also making many things out of wood, rawhide, bark, at camp. Formerly titled Woodcraft. 295 illustrations. 580pp.   21951-8 Pa. $4.00

AN INTRODUCTION TO CHESS MOVES AND TACTICS SIMPLY EXPLAINED, Leonard Barden. Informal intermediate introduction: reasons for moves, tactics, openings, traps, positional play, endgame. Isolates patterns. 102pp. USO 21210-6 Pa. $1.35

LASKER'S MANUAL OF CHESS, Dr. Emanuel Lasker. Great world champion offers very thorough coverage of all aspects of chess. Combinations, position play, openings, endgame, aesthetics of chess, philosophy of struggle, much more. Filled with analyzed games. 390pp.   20640-8 Pa. $4.00

COOKIES FROM MANY LANDS, Josephine Perry. Crullers, oatmeal cookies, chaux au chocolate, English tea cakes, mandel kuchen, Sacher torte, Danish puff pastry, Swedish cookies — a mouth-watering collection of 223 recipes. 157pp.

22832-0 Pa. $2.00

ROSE RECIPES, Eleanour S. Rohde. How to make sauces, jellies, tarts, salads, potpourris, sweet bags, pomanders, perfumes from garden roses; all exact recipes. Century old favorites. 95pp.

22957-2 Pa. $1.25

"OSCAR" OF THE WALDORF'S COOKBOOK, Oscar Tschirky. Famous American chef reveals 3455 recipes that made Waldorf great; cream of French, German, American cooking, in all categories. Full instructions, easy home use. 1896 edition. 907pp. 6⅝ x 9⅜.

20790-0 Clothbd. $15.00

JAMS AND JELLIES, May Byron. Over 500 old-time recipes for delicious jams, jellies, marmalades, preserves, and many other items. Probably the largest jam and jelly book in print. Originally titled May Byron's Jam Book. 276pp.

USO 23130-5 Pa. $3.00

MUSHROOM RECIPES, André L. Simon. 110 recipes for everyday and special cooking. Champignons à la grecque, sole bonne femme, chicken liver croustades, more; 9 basic sauces, 13 ways of cooking mushrooms. 54pp.

USO 20913-X Pa. $1.25

FAVORITE SWEDISH RECIPES, edited by Sam Widenfelt. Prepared in Sweden, offers wonderful, clearly explained Swedish dishes: appetizers, meats, pastry and cookies, other categories. Suitable for American kitchen. 90 photos. 157pp.

23156-9 Pa. $2.00

THE BUCKEYE COOKBOOK, Buckeye Publishing Company. Over 1,000 easy-to-follow, traditional recipes from the American Midwest: bread (100 recipes alone), meat, game, jam, candy, cake, ice cream, and many other categories of cooking. 64 illustrations. From 1883 enlarged edition. 416pp.

23218-2 Pa. $4.00

TWENTY-TWO AUTHENTIC BANQUETS FROM INDIA, Robert H. Christie. Complete, easy-to-do recipes for almost 200 authentic Indian dishes assembled in 22 banquets. Arranged by region. Selected from Banquets of the Nations. 192pp.

23200-X Pa. $2.50